HOPE

OVER

ANXIETY

*How to Smash Crippling Fear
and Live a Life You Will Love!*

A self-help book. A memoir. Your guide.
My journey to wellness. How I found hope and made
my way to having a life I have only dreamed of.

Christopher Moss

This book is dedicated to my wife for
her strength, support and humour that kept
me fighting even through the darkest days.

Disclaimer

My book Hope over Anxiety is meant to guide you on your journey. From crippling anxiety to living a life you will love. It is meant to help you develop yourself into the person I know you can be.

This book deals with a lot of hard topics. It is meant to be inspiring. It is not intended to replace professional help.

This is designed to be informative and educational. It does not replace medical judgments or considered therapy or other higher treatments.

I the author am unable to respond to specific questions or comments about your personal situation, diagnosis or treatment. I am also unable to give any clinical opinions. If you are in urgent need of assistance I would advise you to contact your local emergency services, or local mental health crisis hotlines.

My resources mentioned in this book are used to help and guide you. It is for education and information only. I am not a medical professional. Please do not replace my information for the specialised training and professional judgement of a health care or mental health care professional.

Neither the author nor publisher can be held responsible for the use of the information detailed in this book.

I would highly recommend consulting a trained professional before making any calls regarding treatment of yourself or others.

My promise to you . . . If you follow this book you will . . .

. . . feel calmer. You will have control over your thoughts. You will understand yourself and your triggers. You will be self-confident and resilient. You will be happier and more positive. You will know what life you want and how to get it. You will feel inspired and believe you will be anxiety free!

A challenge to you . . .

You will learn all the skills and gain insight into you. You will be empowered and inspired.

I have laid this book out so that you can become the best you. I would love to see you become anxiety free. It is possible if you follow my book. Are you up for the challenge?

Table of Contents

About the Author

Christopher Moss is married with 2 children. He lives in Northamptonshire, England. He has worked in retail for over 28 years. Currently a store manager.

His first book HOPE OVER ANXIETY is an international best-seller. It's a best seller in 3 countries!

He has a passion for writing, building life skills and inspiring others to take control of their anxiety. His mission is to give people who are suffering the skills and tools so that they can break free on their own. To create a life that they want. To utilise the skills they have from anxiety, to be the best version of them they can be.

The Eclipse

The Eclipse—Richard Eberhart

'I stood out in the open cold.
To see the essence of the eclipse.
Which was its perfect darkness.
I stood in the cold on the porch.
And could not think of anything so perfect,
As man's hope of light in the face of darkness.'

FOREWORD

The Beginning.
Your Path to Hope!

Hello and welcome to Hope Over Anxiety. How you can break crippling anxiety and live the life you will love!

Firstly, I would like to thank you for buying this book. I will show you what anxiety is about, ways of coping, and give you the tools and skills to arm you so that you too can smash the cycle of fear. Like I have.

In the past, I have suffered in silence. Not really understanding what I was actually experiencing. I have had anxiety attacks, but they haven't manifested themselves as typical anxiety, so I have never, until recently, realised what I was facing.

Being anxious, dealing with anxiety every second of every minute of every day is draining. It takes a great will to cope. We are warriors fighting our own internal battles.

We should be proud of how much we have endured and continue to find new and different ways to beat this. That iron will to keep going despite everything will help you in the future like it has me.

So much of my time was in survival mode, just coping with each day as it came, making it through to the next day. When someone says they have anxiety I feel sad for them as I know how difficult it is. I also feel a great sense of admiration. To still keep going, to have the battle scars, physically and mentally but to still be in the fight. That's awesome!

This book isn't too dark or depressing. Some chapters are tough but you can also enjoy a lot of the subjects I will discuss. How I have laid this book out for you as a reader is to see my mindset and be able to take things from what I have done.

I have made this easily understood with no real jargon. I have laid this book out in order for you to follow. There are points you may want to skip and come to later—that's fine. There may be points you want to go over—that's good too.

The book is laid out as simply as possible; a quote, what the chapter is about, visualisation of it, ways to help and some of my experiences. Each chapter includes a brief concluding summary called 'in a nutshell' at the bottom of the page. This not only summarises the chapter but could be used as a quick skim over for those that don't want to read it all. There are a few exercises thrown in as well for you to do.

I have added several break-out chapters—some small chapters designed to make you think differently and inspire you. I have illustrations and words of encouragement all the way through the book.

You will see my battles—how I have struggled. What I have changed to have a better future. This is what I have done to go forward. This is my mindset, my self-talk, these are my experiences.

The book is connected a lot. One skill needed goes hand in hand with another. These skills are simple and easy to understand. This book is here to help you through your anxiety. Like a companion by your side. Cheering you on every step of the way!

I have kept a journal of my feelings when I have my anxiety attacks and their causes. When I first started this book I wasn't totally convinced my anxiety was that bad. Yeah, sure I'd had an awful patch but that's all. Then I started recording details and reviewing them. It totally surprised me and explained so much! My anxiety is far worse than I thought! It has held me back in my career and in love and prevented me from becoming the person I want to be and will be!

I am not a medical professional. This is my first book, the first of many. I have battled with anxiety since I was 10 years old. My wife suffers as does my family.

I have dealt with fear for so long! It has affected my life—31 years!—beginning after the death of my brother, aged just 20 months old, to cancer, and coming to a head two-and-a-half years ago when I was the victim of an armed robbery.

I felt isolated and alone. No one understood my pain. I struggled to get out of my bed and take my children to school. I would have nightmares of his return. Anger, shame, and fear would control my days. I didn't want to carry on with my life.

I couldn't see a way out. I was broken. But not now.

I have researched so much in regards to this illness; TED talks like Alison Sommer, which was moving and informative acting out what a panic attack is like. I had tears and totally understand what she deals with. Neil Hughes' amusing and thought provoking piece on escaping the custard! I have read books aplenty on every part of anxiety, several other books that have explained the human mind, meditation and hours upon hours of internet searches. Not to mention the discussions I have had with other people that experience anxiety.

People have also come forward to share their stories, what they have endured and what they have done to break the cycle. They have shown great courage to talk about their stories, to reveal their inner most fears. I am really proud of them. Their battles should give you hope.

The resilience and strength that we use every day would amaze others.

You aren't alone—many people deal with this. It is a lot more common than you would expect and everyone is different in their day-to-day struggles.

It is okay to feel like this. Take one day at a time, appreciate your progress. Celebrate it. You didn't choose to be like this. It's not your fault. You can break it. You will break it if you follow my book. Imagine that! A life that you have complete control over!

You will feel inspired. So many people try to get out, but can't; others have no hope and have almost given up. I would say to you: keep trying. You will see that it is possible. In the distance, there is a small, but beautifully formed glimmer of hope. Follow it. The possibilities are endless! You can be whoever you want to be!

There are so many different ways to deal with anxiety. I will show you what I have done and a few more that you will find interesting. In order to take on anxiety, you need to believe in yourself, have self-confidence, reach out to others for help and encouragement, and see the good in you.

I still have daily battles with anxiety. I have never felt as good as I do today. I have never felt as alive as I do now! The future is far brighter than it ever has been! So sit down, put your feet up (you have earned it!) and spend a little time reading through and implementing this book.

It's time your anxiety started getting a battering, rather than you. Your path to hope, from despair to happiness and an end to your crippling anxiety, is just beginning!

THE MIDDLE OF THE BEGINNING

My Descent into the Darkness and the Battle Upwards

'The biggest obstacle you will ever overcome is your mind. If you overcome that, you can overcome anything'
—Marcandangel

What is this chapter about?

This is my story of my descent to the lowest point of my life. How I got there. What I did to slowly, fingernail by fingernail, claw my way out of the abyss. What experiences

I have had that have shaped my life up to this point. What steps I put in place to keep growing, and my determination not to go back!

My story—my journey

My journey starts in the middle of the realisation that I was broken. I was suffering before this, but I hadn't realised how bad I felt. I needed this awful moment to shake me up. To see where my life was heading. It was a life changing moment.

12 December 2014 5.55am—my story

It was dark almost pitch black as I walked to work that fateful day, but something felt different, something felt wrong. A part of me was screaming *'go home, go back home!'* I squashed the feeling as I opened the store and entered the premises. The alarm went off as it always did. Then it happened . . . He came at me, attacked me and demanded I opened the safe . . . I was the victim of an armed robbery. I remember shouting loudly *'oh for f**k sake'* as he entered the building. Pushing me through the shop towards the safe. This was the only time I showed any negative emotions.

My life was worth £3,500

I was threatened! Thinking about my wife and children during my 45-minute ordeal had a profound effect on me. I kept it together for the entire time, I was calm but assertive. I don't know where I got that stillness from!

It almost felt like I had detached myself from it. Like when I found out I lost my brother or sitting at his funeral. My emotions for that time were gone. I told myself that it was just an irate customer, nothing personal, deal with him then deal with your emotions. I told myself that my family depended on you. Your kids won't be without their father! My wife without her husband. It is down to you to make sure that doesn't happen.

He wanted the contents of the safe; my life depended on me opening that safe! He demanded I open it even though the timer wasn't ready. He was getting panicked. All for £3,500!

Thankfully I am still alive to tell the tale.

After the event, I watched it on close-circuit. I was holding my hands together, almost in prayer, as I spoke to the robber. I tried to keep him calm and manage the situation the best I could.

I was left physically okay (although I was starting to shake) but the mental damage to me was only just beginning.

I started to organise and get things sorted to reopen the shop. The police sent me home. They could see I was showing signs of shock.

My journey . . . into the abyss

Over the course of the next few days, I slipped more and more into despair. Being at home on my own wasn't good for me. Too much time to think . . .

The previous 6 years hadn't been good; money worries, my marriage was struggling, and my job wasn't great, but this massive event was the last straw, as my nerves took over. That violation had broken me. I was lost before this, but that act destroyed me. I lost what little confidence I had. I lost my strength. I lost.

Facing the person in the mirror

I didn't like the person I had become. I felt I had become too selfish, too self-centred, too closed to my own pain and less caring of others; something in the past I felt I was good at.

Moments of fear and anger would wash over me for no reason. On regular occasions during the day, it would ambush me and take complete control.

I struggled to get out of bed. It was a huge effort. The worry about him coming back and getting into my house invaded my thoughts. I would stay up late at night watching programmes on TV—nothing that I can remember; anything to take my mind away from what I was feeling. To get lost in the show and to escape my emotions. To feel something other than pain.

I would dream of a man completely faceless in black clothing (completely unrecognisable apart from a black silhouette). He would be up against our back window door and opening it to come in, with a hammer in his hand. The feelings of horror, sheer terror and impending death still scare me today and would take hours to shake off after I would wake up.

Other times I would shake with worry. All I wanted to do was curl up in a ball. Every time I looked into the mirror it would hit me. Especially on my own at night, struggling to stop weeping.

Leaving the house was difficult, it had become my fortress. Putting my feet out of the door made me very anxious. But I had to take my children to school; I had to pick them up. There was no choice in my eyes. So I battled through it.

I also felt I had to hide my pain as if I wanted to shield my wife and kids from the dark. I was also being selfish. Without saying how I felt made it less real.

My little dog laying by my side resting on my legs with his warm body was a massive comfort to me during those days. A calming influence. Being forced to look after him and his needs brought about a reach out to real life.

I hated myself, I hated what I had become, what it had done to me. I felt powerless, I felt ashamed. I blamed myself like I always do. '*What if I had not changed my shift that day? What if I had listened to my gut, and not gone in?*

What if I had opened the store differently?'

The days would blur into the next. Some days I felt numb; other days the feeling would hit me hard.

I regularly went to see my GP, but couldn't put steps in place to sort myself out. I didn't want to take medication. I was offered it by my GP several times, but I refused. I didn't know where to turn or had any drive to help myself. The thought of going onto medication scared me. The thought of the six weeks of being nervous and apprehensive before seeing an improvement just wasn't an option! More nervous and apprehensive than I was and trying to get back to work feeling like that? No chance!

There were times I felt that it would be better for my wife and kids that I was no longer around. To stop being a burden, a pain to them. Sure, they would be upset, but long term it would be better for them. No one understood what I was going through. I felt isolated and alone. I wanted to die. But I couldn't do it. What drove me during the ordeal helped me now. I hadn't enough determination to even attempt to do it, let alone actually do it.

I wasn't going to be destroyed. I will strive and do better. It was a massive f**k you to him.

That's how it started, then my outlook changed. My drive was still there, but my motivation was different. I wanted to do this for me. For my loved ones.

To face death—to realise I have a chance to reflect, to understand what happened, to understand me—forced a realisation what I needed to do and do better. I asked myself:

What do I want out of life?

Who do I want to be?—What obstacles will I face?

Where do I want to go?

What can I do better?

How do I get better?—I will get better!

I also felt lucky, others have received worse experiences than me. It could have been far more horrific. I feel this life-defining moment was a gift. I had to change!

My past

When I go back and think about it I have always been nervous and anxious, but the start for me was probably the death of my younger brother Thomas of cancer. He was just 20 months old.

I had chicken pox, and I was the first in our family to get it. What killed him was that virus, as his body was fighting cancer. I blamed myself as a 10-year-old. It was my fault he died. I carried that guilt and pain through my childhood right the way through to my adult life. Feelings of not deserving to be happy, not feeling good enough, deserving all the pain that I was given. I was prone to self-sabotage even if things were going well.

Getting anxious, always thinking of the worst thing that can happen. At such an early age, life showed me the worst thing can happen. I loved him so much. Nothing made me happier than building things with cardboard boxes and sticky tape. We would play for hours in our made up cars. He had his eye removed and had a beautifully made glass one. Seeing the back of his eye wasn't a good experience for me; it was red when he didn't have the glass looking eye. He had a plastic cover instead, and to this day I can't look at people touching their eyes.

I remember going back to school after his death. The world felt different after, sadder, darker. It was as if the colour had drained out of my world. I lost my spark.

I still remember coming home from school, one day, to hearing my mum crying, wailing, squeezing his green babygrow tight for dear life. I still hear that cry, that yearning, that pain. It haunts me. It reminds me my innocence went when he died. Feeling that pain made it worse because there was nothing I could do to mend her hole in her heart. Nothing I could have done to help her.

When we went to visit him, our last goodbye, I looked at his face and body. He looked wafer thin, unrecognisable from the boy I had seen a week previous. I noted the back of his head had been cut where they had done the autopsy. His face and body had a greyish yellow look to it. He looked unrecognisable to the brother that we left when the ambulance came and picked him up. He was so weak he couldn't sit up; he had no energy. What shocked me most was the cold, ice cold feeling I felt when I touched his face. It shot straight through me like a lightning bolt. So cold I couldn't touch him again. He looked so peaceful,l but I just couldn't face touching my brother. I regret never touching him again. I knew that at the time I wouldn't get a chance to properly say goodbye. Just couldn't do it.

Thomas looked so peaceful in his coffin, his yellow cuddles and his favourite teddy bear resting in between his legs. He was such a live wire nothing fazed him. Full of energy, so fun loving.

Some not very fond memories

I hated school. I used to travel to school by bus. One girl a year younger than me, would pin me up against the window with my back held in place. She would take great delight with a big selection of the top of the bus egging her on. My tiny frame was powerless to stop her. Pinned unable to move. Rubbing her boobs on me. She loved humiliating me in front of the others. She got a big kick out of her efforts.

When we went to an adventure week at school, one lad took great joy in picking on people. I was not very developed at school. He, with friends pinned me and pulled my trousers down in front of many kids. They all laughed and it to this day it fills me with shame.

When I was 15, I had a chance of doing well at school and getting my grades for GCSEs, but I couldn't. I freaked out, I struggled. I was so worried I would fail, I couldn't revise. I would spend hours upstairs doing everything but revise. I hadn't the strength to do it.

At 22 I was mugged on a pub crawl. I got led to a park, talking about getting stoned together. I knew that I was in trouble as they escorted me down. They held my hands behind my back as one hit me then they threw me into a tree head first with my hands still held. They demanded my Walkman, pulling a knife and demanding I give them my 21st birthday watch. I refused. I tossed my headphones at them and legged it jumping over a brook, and off into the safety of people. I don't know where I got the speed of thought and pace from. I was too quick for them. I still don't know to this day how I managed to jump that brook but I did.

My chin had swollen up. I looked like I taken the full force of the tree on my chin.

I have always been anxious. I have tried to hide it—from biting my nails to using my smartphone as a safety blanket. I had found that it had kept me calmer, less worried, less anxious. But it also shut me off from life—what amazing life and people I have around me.

I may seem calm on the outside, but I am constantly worrying inside. Checking myself, making sure.

Meanwhile . . . The struggle forward

I got a new job. I will never know how on earth I managed to get through two interviews in the space of a few hours—my anxiety and worry was in overdrive! How on earth I kept it all in I still don't know. All I know is I felt a complete mess! Totally exhausted.

I went to work, but I wasn't better. I faked it. Putting on my best fake smile. I had to go back to work, we had to financially. That was the pressure I put on myself. I needed to get away from that place. From the memories.

It was back at my new job that I pieced myself back together. Little by little. In some ways, it was like starting again at life. Rebuilding. I was determined that this wasn't going to break me. I was determined to do better. I had another chance! Out of all of it, I could make this a massive positive.

To strive to be the person I know I can be. Someone To be proud of.

It was a struggle. I was constantly feeling paranoid and worried. I was going to be sacked, thinking I was going to be back-stabbed by my colleagues, as my trust in humanity gone. Wanting to go home, back to the security of my home. I felt isolated and alone. *Nobody wants you here, you can't do this. You aren't good enough! You are a failure. They will betray you and you will deserve it.* I distanced myself from everyone. Fear of being a failure was constantly on my shoulder.

I started to watch YouTube videos about believing in yourself to rebuild my confidence. I would watch inspiring upbeat clips to help me face the day.

I would look in the mirror repeat my mantras in my head in the morning or if I only had a few seconds I would say *'keep doing better!'*

I started and continue to listen to superhero music to motivate me and make me feel superhuman. I do this most days first thing in the morning. I enjoy the music, but it also helps me to feel inspired and positive.

I then went further. I started planning ahead. Giving myself goals to achieve. Firstly planning, then I started writing it all down. Having goals from the 0 to 20 years.

Things that I will achieve, big dreams. Dreams that I will achieve in my lifetime.

I knew it would take time, little footsteps every day.

I read a lot now, loads of self-help books 'The Gift of Imperfection' by Brene Brown. She taught me to have barriers, what I feel I find acceptable to yourself and to show my vulnerability.

Inspiring books like 'Jobs by Walter Isaacson' and the '4-hour work week by Timothy Ferriss' to name a few, it drives my wife to distraction!; It was reading Walter Isaacson's book about Steve Jobs (the man behind the iPod, iPhone and Mac) that busted open my world. Made me look up at the stars and dream of something greater. A flawed but brilliant man believed that he could do anything! He didn't understand 'no' and believed anything was possible. *'Wow! This man! His team changed so much! What am I doing to make a difference in the world?'* He had no barriers! *What can I do? What have I got? How can I make a difference to people? What are my skills? What experiences can I draw from?* This led me on to writing a book. I want to make a difference to others. I want to reveal my soul so that it can inspire others to seek solace and hope.

Why have I done this?

I have done it so I can be a better father, I can be a better husband, so I can be better. I want to give you the reader hope and dreams of a grand future. I am also making up for lost time. So much time wasted on things that really didn't matter. I massively regret the paths I took. This I use now to keep me motivated.

Over the last 2 years, I worked hard to improve myself. I have challenged myself to improve 1% every day.

I have done this because I want to make a difference to other people, I want to make this terrible experience into something that will help others.

'Life isn't all sunshine and rainbows . . .
nothing hits harder than life'
—Rocky Balboa

It has helped me to reconnect and understand myself, accept myself more now than I ever did. It's okay not to be okay.

I have a journal that I review. It reminds me how far I have come, but also I have planned what I want to do in the future. I am not finished yet what I want to achieve in this life!

This is only the beginning!

This chapter is in a nutshell

- My horrific ordeal of being a victim of an armed robbery took me to my lowest point of my life. It was also a life-changing moment. It was a gift. Not many people have the chance to get a second chance!

- Through this pain I vowed that I will do better. I have now put steps in place to pull myself away from my anxiety and go even further forward.

- I know that it will be a hard slog, but I am making progress. And that fills me with the hope that I will be free!

- I have shown you my experiences to help you deal with your own pain and inspire you to make a change.

How I Felt after the Armed Robbery . . .

The Mirror

Have you ever struggled to look at yourself in the mirror?

To raise your head even to catch a glimpse?

To be petrified to hold that gaze?

To see the person staring back at you?

The broken shell with no soul?

To know that if you held that gaze you would not be able to stop the tears, the cry of a person bereft of hope. Never wanting to stop crying?

Torturing themselves for everything that they have done, all the failures, all the mistakes?

For all the abuse and hurt they have endured in their life, wanting no more. Wanting out?

For already feeling dead. Living each day in hell.

Living for the days when you don't feel anything.

For wanting to smash everything to pieces.

To want to punch the walls so hard that you broke your hands, covered in blood. To feel a comfort in that thought.

To want a release, anything to take back control.

For feeling shame. Like I brought it all on myself.

For feeling shame, wanting to release my anger.

For feeling shame, for not wanting anyone to see me like this. Not wanting it to affect my wife and children.

For hiding all my pain from all that love me.

The mirror doesn't lie. He sees you. He knows what you are thinking. That's why I can no longer look at it.

The Silence

All lights are out.

The darkness envelopes me.

I lay here unable to speak, unable to move.

There is not a sound.

I want to cry but no tears can break free.

I want to scream, loud so loud at the top of my lungs, ahhhhhhhhhhhhhhhh.

I want all my pain and anguish to be released.

I want this desperately but no words come out.

Instead, I lay here trapped motionless, powerless, and unable to do anything but hear the silence.

What is Anxiety?

'You are braver than you believe, stronger than you seem, and smarter than you think'
—A.A Milne

What is in this chapter?

I will explain to you the basics of what anxiety is. What types of anxiety you can have. Some causes of anxiety and some basic ways of reducing your battles. It will give you an insight into what I struggle with.

FACT: 40m adults in America have anxiety (8.2million in the UK) that's 18.1% of the population.

What is anxiety?

Everyone has anxiety in one form or another during their life. From being anxious about a job interview, exam or medical test. These are normal emotional states.

It is when we struggle to control these worries that it then affects our daily lives. For me and many I have encountered, it's like a downward ever more challenging spiral.

You can't escape anxiety once it finds you

I have general anxiety. I find myself being irritable a lot. I find this so frustrating, and it chips away at my confidence. There are times I feel powerless, a prisoner to my emotions. I want to be a more fun-loving, calm and confident human being.

According to WebMD, general anxiety or GAD is 'Characterised by excessive, exaggerated anxiety and worry about everyday life events with no obvious reason for worry.'

Take a recent example. I was driving to a meeting. It was raining, then I started hearing this high-pitched sound coming from my car. *What was that? There it was again!* It was going in a cycle.

I was starting to panic. I have got to get off the motorway and find out. It could be the wheel slowly falling off! Christ, how quickly will that happen? I need to slow down because if it does and I am doing 70, then I am gonna be killed. That would be awful for my family. But there aren't any junctions, oh god! What am I going to do? Each time I heard it the more I panicked and could not think clearly. I was trying not to have an anxiety attack. I had knots in my stomach, I was trying to calm myself through breathing and self-talk, but I was struggling. I could feel my heart throwing itself into my rib cage. Shit, shit, SHITTT. What do I do now? It was then that I realised it was my windscreen wipers squeaking as it had stopped raining! I felt a wave of relief. I felt stupid for even panicking in the first place. But that is my mind, always looking at the impending catastrophe.

I struggle with anything outside my comfort zone or out of my norm. I procrastinate or stick my head in the sand and don't do it. The struggle to actually achieve is a massive battle. This has cost me so much in my life. So many times. Doing the same thing. I can't do it. It's like having to climb a huge mountain. The constant invasive depressing mind talk.

I recently had an anxiety attack worrying about a promotion. I had bought my son a keyboard, for my sins. The music was blaring, my son singing away, trying to get dinner organised, and my wife talking to me. The noise in my head and in the house was unbearable. It smacked me in the face, snuck up on me. I couldn't control it.

I had a tightening in my chest and knots in my stomach. I felt like someone had taken the wind out of me. It was my first anxiety attack for months.

People with anxiety

When I have spoken to people with anxiety, I am amazed how many on the surface you would not expect to have it. How many manage to control it and appear on the outside at least like they are not dealing with anything.

Anxiety has three sides; mental, physical and emotional. Our self-talk is of worry for the future. Emotionally we feel fearful. Physically we are tense.

Fascinating fact—over 70% of your body's systems are used during your anxiety disorder! This explains why you always feel exhausted!

The most common symptoms can be:

- Headaches/pressure—feels like head about to explode

- Palpitations

- Dizziness

- Weak legs—feel like jelly

- Feeling detached from the world

- Tension and muscle aches

- Sweating

- Shortness of breath

- Fatigue and tiredness

- Increased heart rate

- Digestive problems

- Irritable

- Mind constantly racing

This can manifest in a variety of other disorders like:

- Phobias

- Panic disorders

- Post-traumatic disorder

- Social anxiety disorder

- OCD

So many people these days suffer from one form or another. I used to live being stressed every day. It isn't healthy and burns you out. It also leads to being anxious.

Anxiety is an isolating experience. It's overwhelming. It can damage relationships with family and friends and can threaten people's careers and lives. Many people don't understand how hard and energy-sapping being anxious is.

Anxiety is so complex and individual to that person. There are a lot of different types of anxiety like:

Social anxiety – described by NHS.GOV as 'overwhelming anxiety and excessive self-consciousness in everyday social situations' . . .

General anxiety (GAD) – 'Anxiety disorder characterised by chronic anxiety, exaggerated worry, and tension, even when there is little or nothing to provoke it' (NHS.GOV)

High-performing anxiety – High achieving and perfectionist, driven by details and order in a desperate attempt to calm racing thoughts, worry, and the fear that invade every ounce of the mind and body' . . . (Headspace.com)

People can appear to look calm, self-assured, and confident on the outside, but drowning on the inside.

There is no reasoning or logic that can help. Anxiety is purely an emotional state. Most of the time we know what is happening, we understand the logic and battle it, but we feel we have no control over what is happening.

It took me four weeks just to take some rubbish to the local recycling depot. The thought of going made me anxious and fraught with worry. My stomach was in knots. I was scared. It has been one of the few times I couldn't explain why and still don't. I have done it loads of times in the past without problems. This time was different. I had to push myself so hard just to get it done in the end I did it. It only took me 14 minutes to do it. Round trip. I had to listen to Marvel music to inspire me the whole time. Five bags of rubbish!

I felt stupid and ashamed afterward. 'Why the hell did it take you that long? It's only just down the bloody road, you d**k!'

There are days with this book when I have struggled to write—not due to time or other commitments but the nervousness and worry that comes with it.

Is this book going to bore people? This book has to be a beautiful piece of work, it has to! What happens if it isn't? Am I telling them the wrong information? Is this book a clever concept or total crap? Will people ridicule me for showing what my inner most fears and thoughts are? Will it affect my professional career, my children?

Days have been safer not to write. But I want to make a difference to people. The only way I will is by giving everything. And pushing beyond my fears. To show you exactly what is going on in my head.

What can cause anxiety?

Life events – This could be one major event (like me), death, car accidents, for example, or a series of stressful events experiencing many different pressures all at once—relationship problems, work pressures, and financial problems. I have had all of the above.

Self-talk – being on constant guard for the worst-case-scenario to happen. Thinking all of the things that could go wrong will prepare you for when it does.

Biological reasons – It is believed that if someone else in your family is anxious there is an increased chance of you having similar personality traits. I have family that struggle with anxiety.

Evolutionary reasons – Anxiety is an unpleasant experience, but it has also been important for our human evolution. When we feel in danger our body reacts—our heart beats faster to help supply our blood to our muscles quickly, ready for us to fight or run away from dangers. We sweat to cool us down rapidly for a quick response. Both these symptoms are common in anxiety.

Fascinating fact – Eating a banana naturally reduces the effects of anxiety!

Who gets anxiety?

Fact – One in 10 people suffer from anxiety in one form or another during their life.

According to NHS.UK, women are twice as likely to have anxiety as men.

The study was carried out by the University of Cambridge and Westminster City Council.

In my humble view, a lot of men aren't so willing to be forthcoming about what they have to deal with. There is feeling, especially amongst my generation, that men should not be so open with their feelings or show failings.

The truth is anyone can, from famous actors, politicians (some of the most famous of all time) to the person in the street. It does not discriminate.

Anyone can get anxiety.

So many people have experienced it. I read that anxiety is having your own drama queen. Stuck in your head, it is an excellent and amusing description of what anxiety is like. It's your best friend knowing everything about your deepest, darkest, fears and exploiting and manipulating you. Telling you aren't good enough, you're a failure, you are useless and no one likes you.

The anxiety stigma

So many people have anxiety, but the view can be so warped. I don't get why people can say things like 'pull yourself together,' 'it's not that bad,' 'it's all in your head,' 'Don't be such a drama queen.'

What people don't get is that your old part of the brain that senses threats are activated two seconds before your new part of the brain is aware (this deals with rational thought etc) meaning that you can't control the anxiety. It's already there before you have a chance to control it!

For me, it's very real. It can be exhausting and soul destroying. I never asked for this; I never wanted it. I have maximum respect for those that deal with it every day. I am lucky, I know many other people who have worse anxiety than I do.

Ways of reducing anxiety.

Here are a few examples—we will be discussing a lot more in future chapters.

- Get a routine

- Schedule things

- Exercise is more effective than controlling your anxiety.

- Be creative so writing a book, drawing etc has also been suggested to help.

- Mindfulness

Some of the basics

Below is a list of the basics that you can focus on to help improve your anxiety. A lot of these are easier said than done.

- Understand yourself

- Learn more about anxiety—having the knowledge is the first step.

- Learn to challenge your unhelpful thoughts. Try to see things in a more balanced light. I use meditation for this. But sometimes it is still difficult.

- Improve your problem-solving-skills

- Learning and finding ways to reduce your time spent worrying

- Learning ways to be more relaxed

- Learning methods to prevent you from avoiding anything that makes you feel anxious—procrastination my good friend.

You don't cure anxiety. Being anxious has an important part to play in your life, you need it.

We can learn to find ways of understanding your anxiety. Managing anxiety is your best way to deal with it. Fighting head on, trying to control it is probably the worst thing to do.

When you start making changes at the start, it will get harder as up to now you have been just coping with it. The long-term benefits though are more than worth it. To break the cycle needs something different.

Each one of us is different and individual. It is your own needs and the best ways for you that will make a difference. In this book, I will help with that.

A few questions to consider:

What makes you anxious?

How do you think?

What do you say to yourself?

How do you feel?

What are the physical symptoms for you?

This chapter in a nutshell

- Having anxiety is normal, it's when our worries become uncontrollable then there becomes a problem.

- Anyone can get anxiety—you can't run away from it.

- Most common symptoms range from fatigue and tiredness, shortness of breath, palpitations and increased heart rate.

- It can manifest itself into other disorders like phobias, OCD, panic disorders and social anxiety disorders.

- What causes anxiety can be life events, biological reasons (family or parents have it), self-talk and evolutionary reasons

- A few ways to reduce anxiety—more detail will be covered later in the book, such as being creative, meditation and physical exercise.

My Mantras—My Daily Affirmations

'I will face a fear'

'My best is good enough'

'I can't do everything in one day but I can take one small step'

'I will stop and smell my roses'

'Be a somebody that makes everyone feel like a somebody'

My Domian.com

What Are Your Triggers?

'Anxiety does not empty tomorrow of its sorrows, but only empties today of its strength'

—*Charles Spurgeon*

What is this chapter about?

It is about understanding what your triggers are and what YOU experience. I have written down what I deal with. It is a very frank and open account intended in helping you discover your triggers.

My anxiety

I am in a constant battle—an upbeat, positive, joyful and fun-loving person with a depressed, miserable, pessimistic and angry side.

I am very demanding and expectant of myself. I am massively critical and find it difficult to accept anything less than perfect. But, with others, I show kindness and compassion. I put people on a pedestal. I expect too much from myself.

This arrogance does me no favours at all.

To constantly be at a level I have no chance of reaching, let alone maintaining, drains me!

I have to have control over myself and over my day. I structure my time as rigidly as possible. What do I want to do? What are my objectives? And what needs to be done? I get anxious even when things slightly deviate from what I planned.

I get mighty pissed off when I get overruled and we have to follow a different plan. Especially when I know I am right. This adds further weight to my anxiety. Especially when most of the time the plan goes wrong. Only causing me to feel even more anxious, continuing the bad cycle.

I think, what am I doing wrong? Why can't I do the best I can for the day? Why aren't I allowed to do my best?

I get nervous and I struggle to contain my feelings. I use the 7/11 technique (breathe in for the count of 7, breathe out for the count of 11) This is explained further in my mindfulness chapters. Saying to myself, *'your best is good enough.'*

There are times and days where I need to be left alone with my thoughts. I push the ones I love away. I realise that this is wrong and focus again on my breath and say to myself all I need is in this moment. It calms me. I appreciate again what I have.

I also understand now who I am. I am an introvert and I need to be alone at times. I have to have that to get the best of me.

It gets physically and mentally exhausting fighting myself. I have learned a lot more now, to be understanding, and kind to myself. To accept my quirks and vulnerability, to embrace my anxiety.

I feel more relaxed about myself. I am coming to terms with the man I am. To know that others experience what I do and think in a similar way is very comforting to me.

I worry about others. I want to make sure everyone is happy. I notice people's emotional state. Many people have emotional tells—things that show how they are feeling, from a shrug of the shoulders to a curving of the mouth. Worries affect me. I may not show it on the outside. But their emotional state links to me. I have to know everyone is okay.

I get a real kick when I see people happy, to see others progress in their life. I get waves of joy. I want to inspire others to do better.

My anxiety attacks

My physical symptoms—I slur my words, lose words completely. I physically shake, overcome with fear.

- I can get quite petty about silly things. It has to be that way, that's my preference do what I ask. Everything has to be that way. Don't argue, just do it!

- Fast-talking, stuttering, stumbling over words. Or losing a word completely. I am mortified as I stumble further. Then I try to think of the word, and I only feel more anxious and embarrassed. More words fail me. I feel on show I just want to disappear. I feel stupid. This is when I have to do something that I am not prepared for. If I am having to talk in front of others or if I feel self-conscious.

- Going quiet, zoning out and sitting rigid—this has happened to me a few times. When I was under the most stress. This is me at my worst. I have had this mainly at work. I can't stop them, they just come over me. I feel paralysed. I witness the whole thing, it's scary as hell!

- Memory loss—getting things jumbled up. My short-term memory is bad at the best of times, but when I am most stressed, and my anxiety kicks in, I lose important conversations. I can't repeat anything that happened, despite listening the whole time—even things that happened only five minutes ago.

My biggest anxiety

Is not feeling I am good enough—a huge fear of failing stops me from succeeding or doing anything. If it's something I am not confident at, I can't face it. I can't deal with it in any way! I have to really push myself, but I won't be able to do it straight away. It will take several attempts and a lot of positive mind talk before I can attack it. Even then I am fearful, racked with worry. It could be something insignificant like a phone call, or doing something I have done loads of times in the past. The slightest knock will take me back to the start and I will have to do it all over again. The irony to this is that a fear of failure is what motivates me every day.

I have to make absolutely sure I have done enough. I will use my old battered blue notepad and before I have finished my day, I will review and make sure that over 90% of my jobs have been ticked off. If I haven't I worry, I haven't done enough today. I am a failure. This is when my mantra kicks in and I repeat to myself, '*your best is good* enough.' I will need to repeat this as calmly as I can to myself. Whilst breathing through my mouth and nose.

If I have got them all done then happy days, I get a wave of relief, I did it today! I am awesome! I feel good about myself.

Recently I had to go to parents' evening on my own, the worry before it was intense. On went the Marvel music getting me ready for war. The war with myself. It was laid back. It shouldn't have been such a massive thing. But it was . . .*'where do I put my hands, focus on what they are saying, I need to keep everything logged, this is important.'* I was constantly fighting desperately trying not to show my nervousness and worry. Knowing that I shouldn't feel like this, that it was nothing to worry about, only made things worse.

I hate having pressure piled on top of me. I find it difficult. I already have made plans, then to add to them and not enough time to accomplish makes me very anxious. Not having finished all my jobs reaffirms to me I am a failure and don't do anything productive with my day.

I don't sleep well when I have a massive important task. I pile further pressure on myself, putting far too much worry. I tell myself that my best is good enough that it's okay to feel like this. But when I am tired or exhausted this is when I lose control and I can't break it down.

These are getting better. The more confident I have become, the more hope I have.

So many times I will say to myself I will do it tomorrow. Having the intention to do it. But never do. I will procrastinate and will leave it until I have to then force myself with sheer will to get that job done. As always leaving it to the last minute.

There are days when I have finished work for the day, I am so exhausted I can't keep my eyes open, emotionally spent. Needing to recharge—needing to be left alone.

Anxiety at work

It is only recently that I have realised how anxious I was and am. My mind is constantly racing, everything I need to do and manage is flooding through me, what needs doing and what we need to plan. I don't just think about the present. I am also juggling the next few months. My anxiety at work is a huge driving force. That energy has helped me stand out, but it comes at a cost. I come home physically and mentally exhausted, my mind turned to mush. I have a demanding job and I am greatly needed at home but I have nothing left to give when I get there.

Not being prepared, having to speak up to a group or when we get an unexpected visit is when I get anxiety attacks. In the past I couldn't speak. Now I can say things, although I am not always confident sounding as my mind is racing 3000 miles an hour. My mind talk is negative, hammering me, making me feel ashamed.

Take a recent presentation, I wasn't given the information until the weekend before so I had the added pressure of having to prepare for it whilst I was running a store. Already my head wasn't right before I even started planning it. Being completely anxious and fraught with worry.

This led to me in knots on the 1 hour 30 minute drive to the meeting. Knowing how important this was for my career. How important it could be to my family, what benefits I would get if I came across well.

I seem to often drive up the stakes, make it more difficult to focus and concentrate on the one thing.

I tried breathing more slowly, noticing my shaking hands, the tight stomach, the feeling of no control, blind panic and tight shoulders, but it only got so far in keeping me in control. Suffice to say I didn't come across well. I used to be very good at interviews and presentations like this. No longer.

My mind is always way ahead of everyone else as I am thinking about everything. I used to get frustrated with people as they weren't going as quickly as I was. I couldn't get it.

What I expected of myself and the team was unrealistic, but I could do it, why couldn't others? I can get quite frustrated with not being able to get things done and achieving what needs to.

I use meditation to slow my rapid mind and focus on the important things. Understanding the journey and that I am doing good enough relieves me.

There are times that I can use my rapid mind to my best. If we have an important visit from a regional manager or something needs to be sorted, then it can be an extremely useful tool to use to drive me forward to get everything done.

I used to drink loads of tea and coffee. This would make me hyper and crank up my mind further.

Looking after myself

I need my sleep. I need at least eight hours a day. I don't get that my nerves come to the fore. I need to feel refreshed ready for the challenges that face me.

Without my sleep my mind talk is a lot more negative and helps in draining me more quickly.

When I feel exhausted I try to breathe slowly and use the body scan meditation. I will say to myself '*this is me when I am tired*'. This is when I am at my worst with my negative self-talk. Everything is overwhelming, everything is wrong. It is then I distance myself, and push people closest to me away. I deliberately do small things to annoy people so they don't talk to me. I can't cope, I need my headspace. I will do what I need to be alone. This isn't healthy but I have to have it. I am very selfish and tunnel visioned at this point. My wife always calls me a complete d**k at this point.

I hate when I have my anxiety attacks. The loss of words I find humiliating and shameful. I slur my words and have a strong instinct to run away. My breathing is rapid and shallow. I feel extremely uncomfortable it hammers my confidence. I also know I am lucky. Other people have anxiety far worse than I do. I remind myself of that.

I have recently cut back my caffeine intake to just one. I plan to cut it back to nothing. My alcohol intake is pretty much zero anyway. I have done this to help me relax and further aid my recovery from anxiety.

I need my beauty sleep and I won't sleep. I hate feeling exhausted when I wake up in the morning. I can't take on the day like that.

This chapter in a nutshell

- Understand yourself. Know what triggers your anxiety. By doing this you can get a better understanding of what you can do to combat it.

- Take a few minutes to think about your anxiety and how does it affect your day. Write it down. This will help you understand your triggers better.

- Look after yourself. Make sure you get enough sleep, cut back on coffee, tea, and alcohol.

- Be kind and understanding to yourself. You are doing your best. Be fair and look after yourself.

Building Your
Self-Confidence

*'If you don't have confidence you will
always find a way not to win.'*
—Carl Lewis

What's this chapter about?

It is the first block on your path to building your army to
fight anxiety. There are many parts to building your self-
confidence. We will discuss, why have it? How do you
build your self-confidence? Learn to show what you feel
comfortable with and to stop always saying yes to people.

What is self-confidence?

Understanding what you are good at. Having belief in yourself and how you convey this to others. Self-confidence can be learned and you can grow it.

Why do you need self-confidence?

To take on anxiety, you need to believe in yourself, have the self-confidence to reach out and ask for help and see the good in yourself.

Anxiety takes away your self-confidence. With low self-esteem, you think you aren't good enough. It changes you—you are more likely to shy away from going out and what will take you out of your comfort zone, preferring to stay in your safety of your safe box. Short term, this works, but long term, this can shrink your reality even smaller. With less self-confidence you are more likely to feel like a victim. The spiral will continue as your world gets ever more restricting allowing your inner drama queen to become more powerful.

The more you realise being free from self-doubt and more confident, the more you realise that you can take everything that the world throws at you. You can gain knowledge and understanding from any situation. Where there was once anxiety and self-doubt now there is a higher ability in yourself!

How does it feel?

It's like having sunshine on the inside. That nothing can faze you. You feel good about yourself.

By following these simple ways below you too can achieve this!

What do I need to do to find ways of building self-confidence?

- **Forgive yourself.** All the past mistakes and all the things that you feel ashamed of. Let them go. Write everything that you can't accept about yourself—all the mistakes; everything. Throw them away. Having this shame with you will only drain your self-confidence. That pain is the old you. You won't need them where you are going.

- **Set yourself goals.** Start with small ones at the beginning then grow them. Celebrate that success. That's massively important. It will give you strength as you build up to bigger.

- **The quickest way of getting self-confidence.** Get out of your comfort zone. Despite the worry you may feel. I am facing my fears. Anything that gets you doing something you haven't done before. Take on the small battles first. Each time you go through it, your anxiety will lessen, and it will build more confidence in yourself and strengthen the belief you can break anxiety.

- **Self-talk.** Be positive and encouraging to yourself. I know at times this is hard. You are your own worst critic, but, be patient and this will help calm your inner drama queen.

- **Find people willing to help each other.** Building a supportive group. I have listed a few groups and Facebook groups at the back of the book.

- **Exercise**

- **Inspire yourself.** I use Superhero soundtracks like Batman Begins or Man of Steel to get me ready for the day, or take on something that I fear.

- **Learn what you are good at and keep doing it.** Everyone has their strengths. It will bring a sense of fun to you too. Write a list of your strengths.

- **Speak more slowly.** It makes you feel calm. Breathe in before talking. You will be calmer and in control and feel less likely to react.

- **Meditation.** There are several mindfulness approaches you can take. I personally would recommend the headspace one (this is discussed later in the mindfulness chapters). You can listen to and build your self-confidence. Most of this self-confidence building is focused on visualisation, which I love doing.

I have always battled with low self-confidence. I am tired of being seen as the victim. Poor me. I have worked hard to have more belief in myself. I have focused on my best assets. Rather than looking at my bad points and trying to improve them, I have looked at what I do well and developed that.

Learning to accept yourself

I have always wanted to help others, putting my own feelings to one side to ensure that they were happy.

Breaking news . . . no one is perfect. Everyone is human; everyone makes mistakes. So, why do we as people with anxiety give ourselves such a hard time?

Shame is a massive part of being a perfectionist. I want to be clear about perfectionism; it isn't about striving to be better. Far from it, it's about earning approval—which leads me to . . .

Stop people pleasing!

I have spent all my life trying to please. It has made me more stressed and anxious putting other people's feelings above my own. Just to be liked. In this way, it becomes more stress not being you.

By setting out your own personal barriers and saying no, a massive thing for me. Saying no to things that you don't feel comfortable with will reduce your stress levels. Saying no is massively empowering.

- Allow yourself to say no—if they drain you or distract you from what you need to get done. Look in the mirror. Practice it. Say I will think about it. It gives you the chance to consider everything, not feel pressured into agreeing right away.

- What are your personal boundaries? Record what you like and don't like and stick to them.

- Mind talk, you're going to feel anxious, upsetting the person, but if they respect you, they will understand. You will find it will get easier over time.

Understanding yourself

By reading, meditating and having a journal you will understand yourself much better. You will understand what your own personal barriers are and understand for your own health and self-worth it is okay to say no. Trying to be someone you are not only lives to offer you resentment and further increases stress levels and your anxiety.

'The hardest step she ever took was to blindly trust in who she was.'
—Atticus

This chapter in a nutshell

- Confidence in yourself is a skill. Being aware that no one is perfect, everyone has their faults. We think that others are better, but we don't hear their internal dialogue, we only see the surface.

- Confidence has been described like having sunshine on the inside.

- You need self-confidence to develop and go forward. Anxiety robs you of your self-confidence.

- The quickest way of building your self-confidence is to face your fears!

- Building self-confidence can be by stopping people pleasing, having good support, avoid negative mind talk and getting out of your comfort zone.

My Gratefulness Diary and Planning For the Future

'Be thankful for what you have. Your life, no matter how bad you think it is someone else's fairy-tale.'
—Wale Ayeni

What is this chapter about?

To build plans for the future, to have a clear direction. Be grateful for your achievements and see the small things that make you feel grateful. Using these skills will help you in your battle with anxiety. By having tangible evidence that you are progressing will give you the strength to keep moving forward.

Why have a diary?

Without a clear focus, it's like sailing the seas without any direction.

It is a chance every day to sit back and appreciate what has happened during the day. I also have it to clear my cluttered mind; I get anxious when I don't get these jobs done or forget. It is an opportunity to record details your feelings. You can be as open and as honest as you want as it will only be you reading it.

I write special events down; it's great to review them when I want to reminisce. I have also learned to write down day to day conversations, picking up three key points. Forcing me to listen to others more. Because I have to write it down!

I have also noted that it helps you see the funny things in everyday life and the little, special things that occur in the everyday.

By writing down clears my head out. It is therapy for the bad days and the good ones! It improves your memory (my short-term memory can be awful!) and improves my writing skills.

You can assess your mistakes and your successes! Then later you can go back and re-read it. You will be amazed at how much you have changed and developed!

What are the benefits?

Having a diary has emotional benefits to you, it will give you the desire and will to succeed by tracking your progress.

I split this up into three things:

- List three things that you have appreciated today?

- Today I am grateful for?

- What have I done today to help me towards my big goal?

I will then record in my battered blue journal. I do this as a habit five minutes before I go to bed.

Dated 19/4/2017

Three things I have appreciated today

1 – Going out to dinner with my kids

2 – Downtime on my own at home after a busy week

3 – Listening to music while tidying the house!

Today I am grateful for
My family—appreciating what I have. Spending time with them.

What have I done today to reach my big goal?
My book—got 500 words done!

My grateful journal helps me focus for the day ahead and appreciate what I have done. I also have to think what I have been grateful for. Putting me in a positive mood going into bed. Setting me up for the next morning. It also gives me great insight into what is important to me.

I have a weekly plan. I write down in my book and tick off as I go. I mostly focus on doing what I need to do on my days off. This takes me usually 15 minutes a week. On a Sunday.

Usually the first day of the month I will sit down and evaluate my progress from the month before. Then setting up my next month. Using my year and long-term plans as guidance.

It is best to set up your times using a calendar. If you want to use your phone—like I do, or a paper one. Evernote is useful for me to record progress.

Spend time recording your information. The monthly one should only take you 30 minutes of your time. It will help you. It certainly makes me feel less worried. I want to do as much as possible in my life. Putting it on paper and reviewing keeps me focused.

I was given some great advice recently. Write down your goals and put it in your wallet. Often take the small piece of paper out and review it. It will keep you focused. It will remind you of your purpose.

I also have a picture of a holiday destination at work. It reminds me every day what I am striving towards and what goal is important to me.

My family hasn't had a hot holiday for eight years due to finances. Next year we have planned to do it! We will do it!

I would recommend doing the year one at the last part of the year or the first part of the month. Having your five-year and 20-year goals.

It is all about bite sizing your goals, breaking it into manageable chunks.

What goals did I set myself?

My 20-year goals are outrageous. Huge . . . massive. They are so out there to challenge me to push myself. A vision to head for. Keeping me focused. Big goals require significant changes for them to be achieved. So, for example, I am going to help 500,000 people through my book, vlogs and social network.

Life is too short to look back at the end of your life and say I didn't achieve what I wanted to achieve. By giving yourself long-term goals you can break them up into five-years goals 1 year etc. Making them manageable. It also allows me to celebrate my success by putting it down onto paper.

Some of my wishes

- I want to be able to retire at 55. I would love to spend more time at home and write full time.

- Being there for my wife and children a lot more than I have in the past. I want to be able to give my children experiences they will never forget, to inspire them.

- To be able to confidently talk in front of 1,000 people – five years

- Take two courses (how to launch a book and a creative writing course) – 1 in year 1 and 1 in year 2.

- Counselling and mindfulness courses year 3 and 4

- Set up my website, vlog, and Facebook page – Year 1

- Take my family to Paris (my daughter is obsessed with the city) – year 2

- Finish 3 books – year 1 and 2

- Take my family to New York – at Christmas – year 5

- Buy a decent holiday – to go somewhere nice and hot – year 1

- Be able to afford a decent car rather than my battered, but well-used car – year 1

- Be able to spend more time with my family – Year 2

- To buy an iMAC PRO – year 1. A reward for getting this book launched.

- These are a sample of a few of my wishes. They require me to push through my comfort zone to above and beyond. To challenge me and to grow as a person. I also want to do this for my family. They are not rigid and have room for flexibility. More goals and wishes can be added during this time.

What do you want to do?

What are your hopes and dreams?

What are your wishes?

Something fascinating that I learned is that you need people to help you reach your dreams. I have been blessed with so many people willing and wanting to help me. It has been quite a humbling experience. It has spurred me on.

Who will help you?

(Write a list of names who will help you)

Additional—How I used my anxiety against my anxiety to achieve my goals.

I don't recommend doing this from the start. As it will only lead you to more anxiety or panic attacks. Once you have more confidence and control through meditation, I have learned using my fear of failure as an excellent driving force against my anxiety. I focus on what I need to get done for the day. What it would feel like if I complete what I need to get done. Then I focus on what I would feel like if I don't achieve. Telling myself, it has to be done today else you have failed. Giving myself time frames to achieve. I then think of what would be the worst thing that could happen if I don't do it. I get worried and this immediately sets me to action! That fear of failure is an excellent motivational tool to get you to do what needs to be done. Once you have completed a goal, reward yourself. I have done a lot of this in the past, and it did push me. I find it exhausting, but I have achieved what I set myself to do. It enhances where I want to go and reminds me that my anxiety and worry are all states of mind. A warning though. You have to feel in control of the situation. It isn't intended to give yourself a panic or anxiety attack. The trick is still have control and distance over your anxiety.

I am getting quite adept at using my anxiety to achieve what I need. It breaks through my procrastination and worry. But, it comes with me being exhausted and relying on my negative mind talk to keep me going.

This chapter in a nutshell

- Create a gratefulness diary so that you can appreciate all the good things in your day, do this 5 minutes before you go to sleep. It will aid your sleep and set you up for the next day.

- Set yourself clear goals to strive for, make sure they are challenging. I have set myself big goals—the bigger, the better!

- Set yourself daily, weekly and monthly goals.

- The only barriers that you have are the ones that you put on yourself. So keep striving for your dreams.

- Also, put in what good deeds you have done for the day—you should strive to help others, even if it is a small thing.

- By setting yourself goals, this can give you focus and clarity. It has stopped me from procrastinating.

Ruminate:

Over think, obsess about.

Catastrophising:

Irrational thought that something
is worse than actually is.
To worry or panic about the worst thing that
can happen, from any circumstances.
Dictionary.com

Why Choose Mindfulness?

'Awareness in itself is healing.'
—Frederick Salomon Perls

What is in this chapter?

It describes what mindfulness is, an introduction into what it's about. What benefits it gives you. We all have busy lives, so, I have given you a breakdown how I structure my day using mindfulness.

It was on my holidays when I started mindfulness. I had time to form a habit. It usually takes 30 days, but at least my 2 weeks could be my springboard. It felt strange, but taking my dog for a walk meant something different to me. I felt more enlightened. The wind on my face, no one about, the calm . . . quiet. Peace. Bliss.

If the death of my brother was the start of my anxiety and my life become darker, this holiday readdress the balance and took me on a far brighter, hopeful course. This all came down to mindfulness.

What is Mindfulness?

Mindfulness is the practice of returning your attention to what is happening now. Mindfulness does not change reality, but it will improve your relationship with it!!

I feel with meditation calmer, being able to be more detached, given me more control over myself. It helps you have a more positive outlook.

What are the benefits?

So much in life, we are thinking about the past or planning for the future. We don't stop, take a breath, focus on the here and now, and the world that is going on around you.

When I do meditation, it's like a weight gets taken off my shoulders. I feel energised.

One of the most important things I have learned is when I practice, I notice the benefits quickly. I have more energy and feel more joy. The more you practice the stronger you become.

It is all about making it a habit.

Mindfulness, gently and without judgement, help you move yourself to calmer water. Helps you towards the person you want to be. It gives breathing space to your emotions, to see them. To not react as quickly, to be kinder and considerate to others.

Learning the ability to step back from your own thoughts, is an excellent skill, and is key to help you in your battle with anxiety.

I have realised how much my mind wanders—this is perfectly normal and is considered as a default setting, we are always doing it! Our mind is constantly active.

My mind likes to plan for what I need to do for the day, worry about this conversation I had with the person that I didn't handle very well, or reminding myself what jobs I haven't done yet!

I think about the past, all the painful things I didn't do well, how ashamed I am of things I have done. Even small things like text messages, and emails, I will go over and over in my head long after I sent them, *did I word it correctly, and was the tone correct?*

A research study published by the University of Oxford in 2013 found from their online BE MINDFUL course that those who completed it in one month, on average, enjoyed a 58% reduction in anxiety levels . . . ONE month!! That's amazing stuff!

The University of Surrey went further, they showed significant reductions in work-related anxiety:

- 25% decrease in rumination

- 26% in fatigue

- 33% in sleep quality

Mindfulness is not for everyone. However, with stats like that, and my own experience, that's got to be worth giving it a try surely?

Finding the time is difficult, you feel that you shouldn't be doing it when everything is going on. There are days that you feel you just don't have the time to do it, but these stats prove that it can be a massive help and relief. So keep going. Perseverance is key. If all else fails I have to meditate.

How mindfulness helps—what it improves—a few examples

An explanation

Inside the brain behind your forehead, there is the part that figures stuff out. It makes plans, makes decisions and ensures your decisions are acceptable. It is strengthened when mindfulness is practiced.

This, in turn, influences your brain's emotional centre, helping you to be less reactive and understand more than one person's point of view.

Empathy—seeing others point of view

Studies have also shown that mindfulness boosts the part of the brain that stimulates empathy. It also enhances our feelings of love. Giving people a stronger connection of warmth towards others. I have noticed this in myself.

Positive emotions

Another part of your brain is also stimulated making you feel more positive and have a more positive outlook.

Get me out of here!

This is where our problems lie—our old part of our brain helped us when we saw dangers thousands of years ago. This is our survival mechanism.

This perceived threat kicks in before our emotional, and more rational part of the brain is aware, as our senses go through the old part of our brain first.

We have no control; we already perceive a threat before our rational selves can read the situation. This is why people with anxiety struggle. It is how some anxieties manifest. By using mindfulness this part of the brain (the fight-or-flight part) shrinks allowing your calmer rational side to come out. It requires plenty of practice.

This needs repeating . . . by practicing mindfulness, it shrinks the anxiety part of the brain . . . meaning less or no anxiety!!

—That has got to be something to strive for! I certainly am!

What I have done in this book is given you a flavour of what mindfulness practices you can use. There are so many to choose from, from the quick ones to the far longer. There are so many books you can read—I have a mindfulness bible and a few mindfulness books for on the go that I use as a reference, using different things when I need it.

So if you're like I used to be and don't have time to meditate every day, you can plan when you do. Even just a few minutes every so often can have a massive benefit to you. No one has to see you doing it. I call this stealth mode. But it will help you. You can slow down your words—be mindful when you are talking to someone, pause, and each time you begin to speak for example. The options are endless!

It is all about customising your experiences to help you. There are so many different ways of doing it.

You can plan what you want to do or you can read the following chapter on headspace, where the course is planned out for you . . . all you have to do is listen and act.

Before I took mindfulness, I was still in a very dark place. Massive distrust of others, after what had happened and didn't want to be around anyone. But, I have found it has changed me. I have lost much of my paranoia and negative feelings towards others. I am more positive and feel better about myself.

I had a moment one cold, winter, Saturday night, sitting with my family. Covers wrapped over us, dog plonked, as he usually does, on my wife's lap. I sat back and watched taking in the moment. We had had a long, exhausting week; my family was glued to the TV, smiles on their faces! A wave of joy hit me like a veil. I felt pride; THIS IS WHAT LIFE IS FOR! To experience that feeling I hadn't felt for a long time! The last one was when my son was born.

I have had that feeling several times since, little pockets of joy. It re-affirms I am doing the right thing. I am on the right path!

A few questions to consider

Would you practice mindfulness?

What benefit would others have from you doing it?

This chapter in a nutshell

- I highly recommend following a mindfulness practice. This is key for your journey away from anxiety!

- Mindfulness is bringing your mind into the now through breathing and meditation.

- Mindfulness improves your empathy, helps you take far more balanced views and helps you to have more positive emotions.

- Make it a habit. Do it once a day. Thirty minutes are ideal. Progress can be almost immediate. It has been established that it can help within a month with studies showing a 58% reduction in anxiety.

Mindfulness Practice and Mind Talk—Keeping Calm

'I will breathe.
I will think of solutions.
I will not let my worry control me.
I will not let my stress level break me.
I will simply breathe.
And it will be okay.
Because I don't quit.'
—Shayne McClendon

What is this chapter about?

We will go through how often I practice and what methods I use. I have hand-picked some from different sources.

When I first started I meditated three times a week. That was for me resting, headphones in and taking 15 minutes out of my day. Other times I will focus on my breathing or do quick meditations without others knowing (stealth mode). After that I was struggling to have 15 minutes so I instead have broken it up into 3 x 5-minute exercises. Then I had some bad anxiety experiences when life got in the way and I stopped for a few months. I reflected and strived to ensure I ALWAYS without fail have 30 minutes a day for mindfulness.

Every morning. I wake up I tell myself that I will be mindful.

I need to meditate everyday but I have a busy life and I strive to make more time for it. The irony is I get anxious and feel if I don't meditate I will go backward.

A long way from how I used to view mediation. I used to laugh at my wife for using it. Then I tried it!

Prepare your space—I highly recommend finding somewhere that you use that is calm, and going to that place already helps you to be calmer, more mindful. I use my bed.

Being mindful, what I do—

Body scan

How I imagine this one is like a shower, droplets of water dropping onto me slowly, evenly moving from the top of my head down to my toes. I imagine I am in a shower, one of my calm places.

Start off with getting comfortable (laying on a mat or sitting down), quiet, and take deep breaths. Then scan your body starting from the top and slowly move down. Notice how the general mood is today? Any aches and pains. This can take two minutes or ten minutes. It is entirely up to you. Your pace.

Being a Mountain

This is about being calm, strong and determined. Despite everything that may be going on your mind is calm and unwavering.

Find a quiet place. Get comfortable. Breathe deeply then close your eyes. Imagine yourself sitting on a bench overlooking a river. The water licking up against the mountain in the background. It's tall majestic beauty. It's the most beautiful mountain you have ever seen. Unmoving. Strong.

Imagine you are that captivating mountain. You are a breathing mountain. Unwavering in your stillness.

Imagine it's spring and the countryside is alive with blossoms on the trees. The first flowers of spring are out. The sun is beating down and the wind is lightly blowing around you. You just sit watching the world observing everything that is going on. Watching the world as it changes.

It's now a rainy, thundery day. The trees and flowers are getting battered. But you sit watching observing seeing the changes, calm and still and strong. Just like the mountain has always been.

The days change, life changes but the mountain stays, calm and still permanently strong in the face of all.

Anxious meditation

YouTube honest guy – Ease, anxiety, and worry. A real favourite of mine.

Sleep

YouTube guided meditation blissful deep relaxation

7/11

Breathe in for 7 counts breathe out for 11 counts. A good rule also that I am focusing on, is to breathe in for 3 seconds before answering or speaking. It gives you a few seconds to collect your thoughts and makes you feel more in control.

Stealth mode—stuff you can do during your day that no one will know

Mindfully walk

When you are walking around during the day, focus on each movement. The lifting of your right foot. What is your breathing like? Slow down take your time to focus.

Making your breakfast

This is breathing, being aware of what you are doing. Just take the time to focus on your breathing. Being aware of your movements. Notice how it feels, what are the smells you can sense? I highly recommend making it a ritual. Every morning. It will set you up for the day. Putting you in a calm happy place.

Mindfully getting out of your chair at work or at home.

Being aware of the movements you make. Notice them. Do this three times a day.

An additional visualisation . . .

Cloak of protection

This is one I have recently learned. Another layer of protection against my anxiety.

I want you to close your eyes, breathe deeply and become calm. Imagine a cloak wrapped around you. Notice how it feels; safe and secure, calm and in control. Above all else, it should make you feel good.

It doesn't matter what it looks like. It is personal to you only, how it makes you feel. You can imagine what it looks like if you wish.

Practice taking it off and putting it back on.

This may take time for you to get it right. It's there to make you feel good, safe and protects you from unwanted outside influences. Including your anxiety.

Whenever you need it imagine it wrapped around you.

An important thing about being mindful is that it isn't about suppressing your feelings. It's about being able to calm your anxious, rapid mind. To be able to stop, and allow you to focus on the now. It's about noticing your feelings but not delving into them. There are some mindfulness exercises that allow you to focus on your feelings.

When I am meditating

Observing your mind, I find fascinating. You can be focusing staying in the now and your mind is trying every trick in the book to distract you. It's like a toddler pulling you from one thing to the next, throwing everything at you to draw you in. Whether it's getting me to think about a past event or thinking about things that I need to do or bringing up stuff *I have to do this Second!* By noting and observing your thoughts you can get a great insight into you. I have learned so much about how I think. You aren't your thoughts.

Benefits of practicing mindfulness

I am getting to this level . . .

- Increased experience of calm and relaxation

- Higher levels of energy

- Increased self-confidence and self-acceptance

- Less chance of experiencing stress, depression, anxiety

- More self-compassion and others

I have felt more joyful and calmer than I have for a long time. It has helped me reconnect to who I am. To move towards being a better me.

Reading:

This helps me focus on something else, keeps me calm and I love reading about other people's lives. Things that inspire me, things that can help me do better. I have read so many great books. I have had several epiphany moments during this time.

I have read an amazing stat that reading for just six minutes a day, can reduce your stress levels by two-thirds!

Self-talk

I am anxious all the time. I have had a very negative self-talk. From not being or feeling good enough to comments about what I am doing. I now say to myself *'this is me worrying'* and I focus on my breathing.

What has helped me is this. Would you tell your best friend *'Noone likes you . . . you are such an idiot!'* No! Then why are you telling this to yourself?

I have realised how unhealthy my relationship was; it's a battle I am determined that I have to win. I am going to do it with kindness, understanding and to reassure myself. With love and compassion.

I often bring back old events and memories. I relive them or hammer myself for not doing this or that.

I am now aware of myself doing this and simply note my feelings and experience, *'this is how I feel right now, tired, insecure and angry.'*

When I am talking to people and I want to shy away, my flight-or-fight response kicks in. I get nervous and anxious. I say to myself *'All I need is what I have right now.'* I then focus on my breathing. This centres me again. I do this in stealth mode.

My daily affirmations (these are in a break out chapter) I use in the morning and whenever I feel I need to when I am feeling a failure. I will say to myself *'my best is good enough.'*

What my mind does during meditation

At times my mind is like a bucking bronco desperately trying to throw off my meditation. I get agitated, I have to stay with the breath, note my emotion and focus on the breath.

It will try everything to keep me off track. It seems that when I do this my mind throws up job lists I can't afford to forget, ideas for this book, or future ideas.

Other times my mind tries to be inspiring. I get music come to me from nowhere.

I used to find this frustrating and off-putting. By sticking with it, noting the emotion, letting go, it has slowly helped my experiences. You need to do this in the form of curiosity of interest.

I remind myself that I am not my thoughts.

Building my self-confidence

By pushing myself beyond my comfort zone. By reflecting on what I have achieved by going back over my journals and by keeping to my plans, I see great progress in what I have done. I have focused on the little footsteps every day. I have kept the end goal in sight and by working on my self-talk it has helped me rebuild my self-confidence. I reflect a lot on my day. I know I am doing better. I feel less anxious. I feel stronger. But I also know this is a journey. This book has also built my confidence. I am doing things like talking to people I have never met when sorting out this book, I have spoken to people and they have trusted me with their stories. I have spoken to many others I know well and they have shown me a side to themselves that very few others have, to show that vulnerability to me. I feel proud but also humbled that people want to tell me.

Breaking the cycle

Being anxious is continuing to do the same destructive mind talk over and over again. *'You are useless, why did you do that, you aren't good enough, you are a failure.'*

If you have low self-confidence this also makes it difficult to break the cycle. Not feeling good enough, feeling that you deserve this makes breaking it all the harder.

It took me so long to realise that I was in that state. By using my journal, by using my mind talk, I have realised how much I have struggled with anxiety, and how much stronger I am to what I thought I was. To understand how it affects you is the first step. To reach out to others is the next.

It used to make me mentally exhausted every day. The same incessant battle against myself. It was like a war inside my head. I had little left for the outside, my family and work. It's a slow process, but ultimately a rewarding one. Getting my life on to a more even keel. Being more positive being able to understand my anxiety and triggers.

Being able to go forwards. The irony is that by now being in the moment I can now be more positive in the future.

That's what mindfulness has done for me.

Feeling ashamed

I don't react very well when I feel stupid or ashamed. I tend to respond back and try and hurt the other person. As I largely understand others I know what can cause the most hurt.

This chapter in a nutshell

- Meditation has helped my mind talk.

- When I meditate I see just how much my mind wanders and what I constantly say to myself—it is very negative and saps my confidence.

- I have listed some good meditation exercise including some that no one will notice.

- Meditation helps me be more relaxed, have more energy, better sleep, and increased self confidence and less chance of being anxious.

Mindfulness—What Gets in the Way? Practice, Practice and More Practice

---

'It's all about finding calm in the chaos'
—Donna Karan

What is in this chapter?

This chapter prepares you for times when it's going to be difficult to get done. When there simply isn't the time or you feel too exhausted to practice. Or you are thinking 'I struggle with my anxiety already, I don't need to listen to my head even more of the time!' The truth is what's in your head will always be there. The more you suppress it, the more toxic and overpowering it will become when it does eventually come out, and boy will it come out—trust me on that one. The only way you are going to break it is to embrace it. By being mindful to understand what holds you back and break through it.

What will stop you?

Are you too busy? Is there too much stuff to do? Are you too worried that it won't work? Do you feel uncomfortable about doing this? You can sit in a chair or lie in your bed. If you feel uncomfortable about doing that, you can always do this stuff in stealth mode. So, you could be going for a walk. Do it whilst putting the washing out. Or, my favourite, making a cup of tea or coffee. (Making this a ritual is awesome; putting the kettle on, listening to it boil, filling the cup up, smelling the drink, before bringing it to your lips and drinking it slowly. I actually get joy from doing this, my tiny piece of heaven before the grind of the day kicks in. By doing it this way, I get so much more enjoyment drinking it than I did before and it only takes a few minutes more.)

Mindfulness is not just a practice, but an attitude.

Mindfulness works for me only if I am continuing to practice it. There are times that life gets in the way. I have to do it when there is no one about as I won't get the time needed to finish it. It's hard to be calm and in the moment, shut off from the world when WORLD WAR 3 is going on around you.

For a time as I got buried in real life, it has meant that I have stopped meditation; although I continue to do my breathing. It has coincided with my resurgence in my anxiety attacks.

What has stopped me from practicing fully is my circle of frustration. I have not felt calm enough or refreshed enough to sit down and do it. What drives me is my fear of failure, my will to succeed. I want to achieve the best not just for myself, but for my family. They deserve more, I don't just mean more material stuff but experiences, memories, places to visit. Better quality family time. I have not been able to provide for them in the way I have wanted. I recently didn't get a promotion at work. I feel that I have done above and beyond what was needed to fill what was being asked. This has been a huge source of frustration and anxiety for me over the last six months. My patience and understanding have let me down. I have felt that I am not good enough and my mind talk clicks in about failing my family and being a failure. Being in my 40s and not progressing, not providing hits me deeply. This is why I have struggled. It is my worst cycle I have to break, as it's not a case of me doing better. In truth, I can do no more. I can't change the circumstances and the fact in a small part beyond my control. What I can change is what I feel and I need to break this feeling of failure and how it envelopes me and my anxiety.

This is where my mindfulness comes in, not being a prisoner to my own thoughts and feelings but being able to understand what my mind is saying and being gentle with myself.

To start off, your mind is going to be scattered all over the place. You may get feelings of helplessness but the more you practice, the easier it will be.

I say to myself '*this will pass*', whenever I get these feelings.

There will be many struggles, challenges, and distractions for you not to continue your mindfulness journey. '*I will do it later. No time today I will do it tomorrow.*'

The thing that will inspire you and continue your practice will be when you feel the benefits. It isn't a destination to get to, rather being in the now.

It has been scientifically shown that mindfulness practice helps in shrinking the fight-or-flight response part of the brain . . . less anxiety! That can only be a good thing right??!

I get bored quickly, so I need to ensure that I vary what I listen to. Again if I get bored, I won't carry it on.

Mindfulness for me is the most important part of this book. Everything else stems from this. When you get in a better mental frame of mind, then you can tackle everything else.

As a few further words of encouragement

A few things people that practice do differently—

- You don't believe your thoughts or take them all that seriously

- You embrace nature

- You understand all things come and go

- You don't try and suppress your emotions

- You focus on what you are doing—one job at a time

- You are present when listening not judging

- You laugh at yourself

- You practice being curious

- You get to know your true self

- It makes you more compassionate.

Don't be too disheartened if it isn't showing immediate results. Through practice, it will improve your mood and your faith that you can overcome anxiety and become your better you.

It has worked for me. It has given me something I have never had. It has opened doors I never thought possible. I am seeing life, everything from a different perspective.

This requires my time. To breathe to meditate. Then so be it. I can achieve whatever I want to achieve.

The benefits also help others. Your loved ones will appreciate a calmer, fun-loving-person.

This chapter in a nutshell

- There will be times you will struggle to practice. These are the times you will need to do so more than ever. Even for a few minutes at a time. Those pauses are priceless.

- Find ways to continue mindfulness, even if you can't meditate. You can take walks, talk more slowly, do stealth meditation, do them at work—there are so many options!!

- A few words of encouragement. It has been proven that it helps. With the right attitude, you will be able to continue practicing. And a better way and life beckons!

My Trip to Brighton and an Anxiety Attack

When my anxiety takes control.

When someone mentions that they have an anxiety attack, so many people think they are curled up in a ball, crying, struggling to breathe. Nothing in my case can be further from the truth.

I am an introvert. The thought of sharing a room with loads of people I don't know is daunting enough—but sharing a small space, crushed up against people I don't know is a whole other level of anxiety!

We were on our final leg to our journey. Other trains to Brighton had been cancelled. The driver advised over the intercom that other people should take the next train to our destination. There were only eight carriages and loads of people going to one train. Bedlam ensued. Everyone crammed into one space. Several stops having to turn people away as everywhere was packed. There was no space at all. I was worried about where my kids were. Was my wife okay? I was worried about if we lost our bags. I was pushed up against my wife. I had my hands on the railing gripping it for dear life, my legs spread out. I was stretching and not in a comfortable position. My mind was in overdrive. 'We *could have a crash, someone could steal our kids, wallets, and bags.*' I felt that I was protecting my wife from all the pushing and pressure. The pain in my calf was unbearable but the pain kept me focused. I could feel the anxiety cranking up. Feeling powerless. I was mortified trying all I could to stop the anxiety attack happening. I was frantic. But I hid it from my wife and kids.

I was doing my 7/11 focusing on my pain was an anchor point. Keeping me from feeling powerless. 'Please not now, not in front of these people. Fake your calm, fake it's okay. Focus on what is going to happen this week. What fun we are going to have. Finally away with the family. The children have been so excited about this! Don't let anyone see you like this! Calm. Still'

I was commanding myself to do it . . . demanding myself to not fail. All my will.

I felt my heart pounding. All I wanted to do was curl up. I knew I couldn't. I felt my emotions taking over. I kept breathing; kept fighting it. I felt my emotions were going to overcome and to swarm over me. I was quiet to others as inside my battle continued. '*You can have a moment later. Now you can't!*'

The worst feeling I had was being scared. Massive fear of completely making a fool out of myself and embarrassing my family, feeling humiliated in front of my kids. I know I shouldn't have felt that way, but it was a very real worrying state for me to be in.

I did have a few minutes earlier. Tears in my eyes, breathing hard. Away from everyone. I felt I had been hammered for days by Mike Tyson.

I still had to find the energy to take our bags across the town to our hotel. I shut off, went quiet, and went into my own world to replenish and to distract myself.

I pretended I was okay, it was the worse anxiety attack I had for years.

I hate not having control, not being able to do anything, feeling completely powerless. Just holding everything together, not to show my suffering for dear life. I really didn't want anyone seeing me that way so it all happened without any of my family noticing.

Headspace—What It's Done for Me

Getting myself back on track

After my experience at Brighton, when I had a full-on anxiety attack, I vowed to make changes to my day. It was the final anxiety attack I have had during that period, one of the worst ones I have ever had. It was a massive wake up call and fear of slipping into my dark past motivated me to make changes. Reaffirming my determination.

There was no way I was going back!

I had stopped meditation, I had stopped being mindful. I felt that my anxiety had improved, I don't need to continue the practice.

First thing I did was to make sure that I meditated everyday—it had to be a habit, but it needed to challenge me and not feel boring. I quickly do with the meditations on YouTube. They needed to build me up, take me on a journey. So, what I decided was set my alarm for 20 mins earlier and start meditation before I get out of my bed, starting the day with that intention. Then have a couple of 5-minute ones at dinner time (YouTube) and then the sleep one at night.

I have used Headspace in the past—the free version—where you can do the basic course for 10 days, but, by paying (works out at £60 a year) there is an anxiety pack for 30-days. I find Andy, who does the guided meditation, easy to listen to. He gives you a good pep talk to start when he is in the meditation, he will get you into a routine, and over the course of the 30-days give you little things you can do throughout your day.

I have meditated for over 35 hours now! I have now done 4 courses. It has made me calmer, more caring of others and I see more blue skies now than I ever did. I need less sleep, I have higher energy levels, I have been far more creative at work and I am giving more time to others, which I am very much wanting to do more of. Am I cured? No, not yet but I am certainly getting closer to my goal of being anxiety free. I feel I am not far off now.

Without doing this I would still be struggling.

Without making these changes, during a difficult period of my life, I fear that I would have got worse again. It was certainly heading in that direction before I made changes.

I intend to develop my meditation moving onto other 30 day courses such as relationships and health.

I have vowed to meditate every day WITHOUT FAIL . . . NO EXCUSES! I have put this above anything else, in order for me to function. If it means I don't write, or miss time on my phone or a couple of my TV shows then that's the price I need to pay.

I have no affiliation with Headspace, I highly recommend it. It removes the need to plan out your time. My most precious commodity.

It allows me to listen to an expert guide me through my course. To build the level up as you go (he splits them into three ten-day sections) you can also do single meditations (like walking and sleep) and you can track your progress! That's a big bonus for me. Seeing how many days I have meditated only encourages me more.

My Hope

I remember a time when I felt I deserved nothing but pain.

I hated myself and wanted to push everyone away.

I felt guilty when things were going well.

Expecting disaster to strike or doing all I could to make it happen.

I felt a cold shell aimlessly trying to survive me. Looking for battles in all the wrong places. Expecting all my loved ones to let me down.

This is before I found hope.

I can now look up at the sky and be privileged to be able to see the beauty in the world.

To touch a rose petal to feel its softness and strength.

To feel the lick of the wind during a hot summers day.

To watch with joy seeing a bird soaring, riding the sky.

To look up at the sky and see the wonder in the clouds. To be amazed.

To see the world as it should be.

To know the challenges and struggles I will face but know they will pass.

To know my anxiety will be good on some days and bad on others. To be okay with that. To know I will be anxiety free.

To know I will get better and stronger. To see how far I have come in such a short period of time.

To feel joy Intense, amazing and moving.

To know fear but know it will no longer hold me back.

To look in the mirror hold my gaze and say I am okay.

To have so much love and hope for others. To want people to grow, and take real joy in their happiness.

This is my hope.

This is me now.

This is my soul.

What My Day Looks Like

Mindfulness and cramming it all in

I try and regiment my day, pack everything into it. There are times I have to multi-task. Both I and my wife have very demanding and exhausting jobs. We both have to be very focused to ensure everything gets done. With the added challenge of having two children!

I need to structure and get the most from my day as I can. I do have some wiggle room in my time slots, as there is always something that gets in the way or problems that need to be dealt with.

I have done this to show you how I structure my day— what I do can give you an understanding of what you can to achieve. There is nothing in here that is daunting. I haven't put in the other stuff that I do—the basics like phone my energy company etc.

6.30 Get up and meditate in my bed. Put my headphones on. Sometimes I don't think my Headspace is enough, so I will go to YouTube and find an inspiring five minute guided meditation, to put me in a good mood.

6.50 Take a shower, I have a few minutes to think about my day and have my breakfast—will have my first cup of fruit tea. Try and get time to have a tea, doing it mindfully (no caffeine as cutting back to help my anxiety, I really love the fruit teas . . . chamomile and ginger).

7.00 Take my dog for a walk around the block. Look around at my surroundings. I live near to some woods, the birds singing and the sun coming up is a great sight, sets me up for the day.

7.15 Tidy the house, put the dishwasher on and washing machine on before saying good bye to the family and dropping my son off at school.

8 am Work. During my break, I will go for a walk if it's down to get something to eat or I will sit in my car. Seems the only place I can go so that I won't be disturbed. I need this space every day. If I am in the office I will be constantly hassled. I need to be left on my own to recharge, and to keep my mind calm and clear. If I haven't meditated I will do so now. Headphones on and calm. I find this difficult as I don't like the thought of others watching me. It's in this time that I will do more of my book.

6.30 Usually around this time I go home—brave the busy roads. Have my dinner. Switch off from work. Try and have a chat with my wife and children.

7pm Take my dog for a walk. It has become so regimented that my dog is already telling me that he needs a walk when I have almost finished my dinner!

7.30 Prepare uniforms and lunches, tidy the house then get the kids to bed—usual chaos and bedlam ensue. I do try and have five minutes with the children then. Just me and them. Something that both insist on having since I introduced having a one to one. It seems to be a great way of connecting with them and talking about their day. They always ask me first about how my day was!

8.30 Spend time watching tv, reading, writing this book and talking to my wife. If I get a few minutes I will read.

9.30 Fill in my gratefulness diary. Listen to Headspace on sleep, fall asleep, exhausted.

Repeat every day—to infinity and beyond.

Obituary

'You were put on this earth to achieve your greatest self, to live out your purpose, and to do it courageously'
—Dr. Steve Maraboli

One of my favourite films is Saving Private Ryan. It has a moment at the end, near the end of his life.

He kneels in front of the grave to the leader that saved him during WORLD WAR II. Weeping, his last words before he died next to him, were simple 'Earn this, Earn it'. Thoughts going through his head that his life has to be special, that he has to be the very best version of himself. Not just for him, but for all of those that gave their lives so he could have his.

He talks about hoping that he has had a good life. He says to his wife 'Tell me I have lived a good life. Tell me I am a good man.' It's a moving scene and I use it to inspire me. I am here for a reason, just like every single one of us is. I want to earn what I have in the past taken for granted. Life, being lucky, having my health, having a loving family.

Writing your own obituary is a bit morbid, but it is also essential to focus and give you a purpose. A life purpose. What do you want from your life? What is your purpose? What do you want to achieve? Life is so short, time is a precious commodity. I want to achieve so much. I want to make a difference to people. I want to achieve what I have set out to achieve, as I am driven and determined.

At the end of Titanic when the camera pans across, all of Rose's achievements are shown. I want to make sure that I have had a good life, I have completed all the goals I have set myself. Making some amazing experiences that they will hold for the rest of their lives and shared with the people I love most dearly—my long-suffering wife, my children and the rest of my family. I want to have utilised to the best of my ability, all the skills, learnings, and personality I have been given. This is a massive challenge, one I am up for. That's my ambition. That's my legacy.

My obituary if it was now . . .

We are saddened by the passing of our father and husband. His bland cooking and soul-crushing pasta bakes had even the stoic of stomachs running for cover. He passed having done a bit of stuff, not achieved much and focused too much on his job.

He was married for 15 years leaving 2 children.

My obituary as I want it to be . . .

We are sad to announce his passing in his sleep. Leaving his 99-year-old wife. Surrounded by his grandchildren. His list of achievements includes being a qualified counsellor. He has travelled the world. Having some amazing experiences, the chocolate-loving, storytelling, fun-loving old codger leaves a legacy. He helped so many people in his life. He gave so many experiences to his children and many fond memories.

Then drop this to just 20 words or enough that you can remember and recall with ease. This is your vision, what you aspire too!

To give yourself a purpose. A reason it fires me up. I want to be the best me I can. I need to feel productive, to achieve what I want to in my life, and to make up for lost time, every moment has to count.

My 20 words . . . my vision of what I want to be.

To inspire others, to reach out to 500,000 people. Travel the world. To be a man my family is proud of.

Now it's your turn!

Write your obituary . . .

Break it down to 20 words . . .

What are your barriers? What is stopping you in being a better you?

What is your life purpose?

I want to make a difference to others, I want to be a husband, son, and father to be proud of.

I want to inspire others, to help them find their way out of anxiety, to push themselves beyond what they could feel possible, to be their best!

I want other people to feel comfortable, inspired, and joyful around me.

I want to push beyond—way, way beyond—my comfort zone.

I want to break my challenging goals then set up even harder ones!

I want to be the very best me I can be!

I want to give my children the best life possible.

I want to give my family the best experiences I can dream of.

What is your life purpose?

What Is Your Perfect Day? What Life Would You Love?

What I want you to consider is what it will feel like, what you would wish to be your perfect day? Something you can dream of and strive to achieve. And, what is getting in the way to achieve this? Be inspired to push yourself beyond, see your dream become a reality!

Wouldn't that be amazing?

What would happen if you actually achieved this! Just think about that for a second.

I am sure that you are reading this and saying, no chance! There is absolutely no way that this will happen. EVER! What I will say to you is this—You have come this far, daring to dream, pushing your own barriers, giving you that confidence and belief. Hope will give you the confidence to live your best life. What you dream to achieve.

It could be as simple as being able to go down to the shops and spend some time with your friends.

It could be travelling to another country.

Expand this. If you can dream your perfect day, what could be the life you will love?

Consider the next few questions . . .

What will that feel like? Then I want you to write down.

WHAT WILL YOU DO?

How would it feel getting up symptom-free?

Imagine and write down.

Imagine how you would feel about life?

Imagine what your home would look like?

Imagine what would you love to do?

Imagine what your friends would be?

Imagine how your perfect day and life would feel?

DARE TO DREAM, you might just surprise yourself!

Anxiety and Being Creative

'Anxiety is part of creativity, the need to get something out, the need to get rid of something or the need to get in touch with something within'
—David Duchovny

What is in this chapter?

How you can cope with anxiety by being creative. By letting your hair down. By having fun! You can pick and choose which ones that you would most like to do. Being creative in itself is its own therapy!

Why be creative?

Being creative helps to reduce stress and anxiety. I like to write, but there are so many other things that you can do to help.

What things can you do?

You can listen to **music**. Put on your favourite album or song, crank up the volume and listen!

You can do this when you are getting the dinner ready or when you are getting the kids' lunches and clothes ready for the morning or taking the dog for a walk. It gives you a buzz—depending on the music, it can also be soothing. I always feel a little happier after putting a good song on.

Painting

Drawing and sculpting can help you visualise things that may feel hard to put into words. You feel safe whilst visiting a past experience, trauma or a difficult time. The sense of touch as you grow an idea, can feel rewarding and build your confidence. Painting allows you to do something positive by challenging you and achieving artistic goals. Channelling your focus. Like photography. Seeing something come alive as you paint is a great joy.

Dancing

Dancing, tai chi, and yoga are apparently good. Physical work of the mind and body helps to release stress and anxiety. People who do this report improvements in their quality of life, body image, and self-awareness. They also feel they have better sleep.

So, whether you want to go to a class or just go out and enjoy it, then there are plenty of options available to you. If you don't fancy that then how about doing what we do? After a pretty stressful week, we will put the music channels on dance and have fun as a family. It cheers my family up no end.

Some people say that it gives them a sense of purpose, makes them feel like they're doing something productive rather than obsessing on worries and fears.

Also by using repetitive patterns, it gives your mind a rest whilst you can use your artistic side to create beautiful patterns.

Most of these things for me I would struggle with. I love listening to music, to lose myself in the song, but my creative side is in writing. I can't draw or paint, I am poor at it. If you are like me then why not buy an adult colouring or mindfulness book?

Creative writing

All you need is a pen and paper. Recording your traumatic experiences has been proven to show improvements in physical health and a boost to immune systems. Writing your feelings can help your pain and anxiety. Writing a journal has been linked to self-growth, spiritual awareness, and creativity. I have covered my gratefulness diary and my plan in another chapter. I personally highly recommend doing this.

You can also use poetry. I have read some beautiful poetry describing their pain and suffering. It helps to relieve the pain and it is therapeutic. I love writing poetry.

Cooking

Cooking is also another great idea. Having fun with it. Experimentation with different foods adds to the fun. Getting others involved also is great and further enhances the joy of cooking. Make it an event. Invite people over and have a good chat. It's also another great way of getting out of your comfort zone.

Daydreaming

Daydreaming can help you in so many ways. It can solve stressful problems, it relaxes you and inspires creativity. Doing this also helps to calm you. It has helped me come up with some ideas for my future books. Being in daydream mode is when you are in your most creative place. I highly recommend setting aside time to daydream. You will be amazed what comes out of your head!

Creativity is in every single one of us. Most of us never use it or get the best out of it. It allows us to develop personally and professionally, to view problems in a different way, and use different parts of our mind that previously we may not have tapped into. The confidence I have got from this has been great. Even just having that sense of fun or something to look forward to, is a great help to me, and will be to you.

Intuition

I also learned that over the last few months my intuition needs to be listened to. I used to get this mixed up with my anxiety, but I have learned to understand my intuition—my gut is a very perceptive, powerful tool. So many times my gut has told me 'no', I have ignored it to my peril!

There are times when some random idea comes to me. Whether it is a future idea for a book or character or something I can do at home. I use Evernote on my phone and jot it down. I have sections in there that I cover for most of that.

This mind dumping is important to me. It allows me to clear my mind. I don't have to worry about it and can carry on with my day.

Getting into the zone

When your juices are in full flow, you have got your head down and you are creating something amazing. Time stops, your mind naturally removes your anxiety and sense of time.

The more you get better at what you are doing, the more times you will get into the zone. Meaning more times that you will feel a natural reduction in your anxiety. Can't be bad, can it?

This chapter in a nutshell

- By being creative helps to reduce stress and anxiety.

- There are several examples of being creative such as writing, painting, sculpting, and dancing.

- Doing something creative gives you a sense of purpose.

- The more you practice, the better you will become. The more times your anxiety will naturally drop. As you get into your zone.

My Best Fake Smile

Fake it till it's real

We anxiety sufferers are mostly good at this. Hiding our pain, making sure that no one sees the hurt.

We make sure everyone else is okay, we don't want to cause a fuss, and we don't want others to see us as anything other than fine.

I put this front on for a long time. My most challenging period was once I was back at work, after the armed robbery.

Trying to keep this facade up was draining in itself, but I had to fake it. I didn't want others to see me like that. I feared it showed me less than I should, like I was weak, I was a failure.

The anxiety, the paranoia, the lack of trust in anyone drained me, everything was draining! I was in a constant tormented loop, day after day, and it was getting harder to keep the facade up . . .

I faked it in front my family—my wife, my friends, my work colleagues—everyone.

My stubborn arse refusal to admit defeat. To say '*I need* help.' To show my vulnerability. That arrogance to believe I don't need anyone else's help because I am different, and the rules don't apply to me! I kept the facade going on, for far too long.

I felt that I could lock myself away, I could hide me until I could fix me, on my own. So that no one else could see me in this humiliating state.

I don't need anyone else, no one else could help me, and no one else understands what I am going through!

I shut myself off from everyone, even those closest to me. My wife, mum, dad and my family.

I thought that distance would give me time to fix me. They didn't want to hear me moaning, going on about the same issues. Hell, I didn't want to go on about it anymore, why the hell should I put them through that too!

The thing is though, that best fake smile can only last for a short time. Your loved ones know something is wrong when you stop talking. When the facade cracks—and it will, the dam can only last for so long before it bursts. The iron will to keep it up can't last, it won't.

The best thing that you should do is step out and ask for help, to get help, to realise this is bigger than you can carry.

You would be amazed how many people suffer from anxiety, you would think so many people that have it don't seem to suffer and they look as if they have their life sorted.

One of the greatest strengths we humans have is the ability to help others as a group. The compassion that love and support for a fellow sufferer will help you realise that you can lean on others. That you don't need to suffer alone. No one should.

Show that fear, open up and see what responses you get. Everyone is loved. Everyone has a massive part to play in other people's lives. No one should feel that life isn't worth living. That no one would notice or care. They will notice, they would be devastated. They want to help.

So drop that fake smile, let the world see your pain, let it out, lean and support others and watch what happens.

Because you might be surprised what happens next.

Investing in You

'Investing in yourself is the best investment you will ever make. It will not only improve your life, it will improve the lives of those around you.'
—*Robin S. Sharma*

What is this Chapter about?

This is about looking at yourself, thinking about what you want to do. Are there any skills you would like to learn? Is there anything you would like to do to develop?

By looking to the future gives you focus. Improving you improves your confidence, builds your hope and aids in your recovery from anxiety.

Why invest in yourself?

You are probably thinking what does investing in yourself mean to someone that is crippled with anxiety?

By improving yourself you will help you feel better. Not only will you see an improvement now, the benefits will continue to come into the future. Like most things in life, it is about practice and ensuring you take that time. I know that there are a lot of times during the grind of your day you can get so focused on what is going on. Spending this time can give you a massive lift—something you can look forward to, more confidence and an extra spring in your step. I don't just want you to feel better about yourself now, I want to give you a better future.

There are so many theories around how to improve yourself. Some self-help books will say focus on your weak points; others will say just focus on your two best skills. It's down to personal preference. I know my faults, I can be grumpy especially when tired, I need my own space and when I am stressed I take it out on others.

I personally think that you should focus on your two best skills and work on your one worst fault. I want people to be flawsome, accepting of their flaws yet still shine!

Write a list down of your strengths here—you know you have them.

Dosomethingcool.net has 5 ways to invest in yourself

Simply put . . .

1 – Learn more

2 – Find more free time—a lot harder than you would expect.

3 – Achieve goals—set a plan

4 – Become healthier

5 – Save more money

- Listen to your intuition. Listening will make you make better decisions. Valuing and listening to yourself is very empowering and develops your confidence.

- Invest in building up your confidence.

- Focus on the happy aspects of your life. Everyone wants more, strives to get more. Being happy is a choice, a way of life. It is always important to appreciate who you are and where you have come from. Celebrate you NOW. Be excited to see what you can do in the future!

- They say that 10% of your money should go on yourself. So if it's a good book or a course it is important to keep your skills and keep improving. Always look to improve who you are. That investment will pay dividends in the future. I promise.

Matthew McConaughey in his Oscars speech said that when he was 15 he was asked who his hero was. He thought about it and said my hero is me when I am 25. Then at 25, 35; meaning he always has someone to strive, to chase. You should never compare yourself to others. It's about making you better. No one has your sets of skills, no one else in this world has your personality, outlook on life, and you are unique! Only focus on doing better for you and your loved ones. That's what I am determined to do!

There are courses I have planned to do this year. I want to complete at least one course. I also want to go on a creative writing course.

I want to go further. I want to be able to talk in front of 1,000 people calmly and confidently. The thought of doing this sends my anxiety sky rocketing. It's a huge barrier, one that will require more strength than I have currently. It will require more self-confidence than I currently have. Another reason why I have chosen this challenge! It will be another milestone in my progress. It will mean I am more confident, more comfortable with myself and have less anxiety! How about that for a challenge!

Looking after yourself

Knowing your limits—we are all human. So not having enough sleep, doing too much physical work, expecting too much, putting too much on, and expecting to be perfect.

I need to take this advice because I often push myself beyond my limits. Well beyond. To the point of falling asleep at the table when we are supposed to be having dinner, or having nothing left to give my family. Anxiety robs me of much of that, but I don't look after myself enough either.

Make sure you are eating the right foods. When you feel ill, go and see your doctor (I, like most men, are terrible at this) getting plenty of fruit and veg, that sort of stuff. Cut out that sugar! Many people with anxiety will look for a sugar fix, I certainly do, to keep going forward with your day. Short term it helps but long term isn't a good idea.

- Have a haircut, get some nice clothes. I am not suggesting to go overboard, just doing this every so often. Looking after yourself, for me, gives me a confidence boost.

- Do things that relax you. This could be anything. Books, for me, have helped me learn more about myself. It has made me realise that for too long I have suppressed my creative side. And has taken me on a journey of self-discovery. It has made me more confident and more knowledgeable. Reading books also helps to release stress.

I will try and cram in as much information into my day. So if I am taking the dog for a walk or listening to an audiobook that will help me, then I will do it. I find these also therapeutic. Knowing that it continues taking me forward gives me the motivation and spirit to continue striving forward.

For you to be the best you can, you need to make sure that you are in the greatest shape. I have some work to do on this as my downfall is chocolate and coffees. To give you the best chance you have to think differently and look after yourself. I gain confidence from feeling better and doing right for myself.

By improving yourself, by doing things like courses you enjoy and reading books you will see progress in yourself and naturally you will feel happier and confident. This has happened to me. Without taking more time on myself I wouldn't be on this path now.

This chapter in a nutshell

- To invest in yourself gives you the opportunity to be the best you that you can be. This will drive your confidence and self-belief.

- 10% of your income should be invested in yourself.

- Learn more, find more free time and achieve goals you set yourself. Ensure they are challenging, but achievable.

- Look after yourself—know your limits in order to be the best you can be. Make sure you get enough sleep, don't drink too much caffeine. Eat the right foods.

What Reading Is to Me!

I love going into bookstores, not necessarily to buy but to feel the environment, the calm, the endless possibilities that every book has hidden under its covers. The inspiring words, the hope, the treasure that can unlock another secret door in me. A hidden treasure that would inspire me that would help me on my journey.

Going on Amazon, looking around for new books to read, I now have a list to buy to keep me going with. The list is now 30 books and rising. When it comes through the post it's like treasure. It's a ritual I have, touching the cover.

I need to read. I do a lot of it. I get anxious when I don't get the time or life takes over. I have pledged to read 30 minutes a day minimum.

It frees my creative mind from the shackles of my job, my expectations, everyone. I feel calmer, inspired, it puts me in a good mood.

It has given me a chance to discover who I am.

I think differently to others, more out of the box. I feel it gives me an edge at work.

Why read?

It's a chance to escape, a chance to see the world through another person's eyes. To understand them. It gives you a chance to learn and grow. It can challenge your opinions of the world. It has also been proven that people that read fiction books have better emotional intelligence. Not any other form has stimulated, inspired or given me that epiphany moment.

Books I have read that have inspired:

- **Steve Jobs – Walter Isaacson**. He was given total control and access to anyone he wanted to talk to about Steve Jobs loved ones and enemies. The book is a brilliantly insightful look at a flawed genius, the ability to show us the future, to make people believe anything was possible! It certainly did that for me.

- **Quiet – Susan Cain**. 7 years in the making. I discovered a lot of who I am. I am an introvert. I need to find my 'restorative niche' (time on my own, I have made sure I take at least 30 minutes a day alone) the fact that there are millions of people that are similar to me was comforting and inspiring.

- **Reasons to stay Alive – Matt Haig**, an original, brilliant book on anxiety and depression. I have read several books on the subject and not felt a connection an understanding from the author. This one is inspiring, humorous, insightful and original it has been endorsed by every actor possible.

- **The gifts of imperfection – Brené Brown**, showing your vulnerability. Building your confidence. Understanding that you are not perfect and that's okay, that's good. To show this brings people closer to you. To not feel bad about saying NO!

Music That Touches My Soul

Music, I love. You want to be inspired. To be fired up for the day. This is my play list!

- **Dark knight** full eight minutes – Hans Zimmer at his brilliant best

  It pumps me up. I can relate to the music it is my battle with anxiety, it gives me the belief and will to take on the day.

- **Sunshine Adagio in D minor – John Murphy** beautiful and inspiring piece. When I am feeling down this lifts me up.

- **Time** – inception dark, brooding music listen to this on my headphones. Love listening to this.

- **Baker Street – Gerry Raffety** (long version) the guitar solo is the most beautiful piece I have ever heard! it touches my soul, gives me joy. The whole song is brilliant, but that solo. WOW! By far my most favourite song of all time!

- **Walk – Foo Fighters** I can relate to the lyrics. 'I think I have lost my way, getting tired of starting over.' My anxiety song.

- **Comfortably numb – Pink Floyd** again, a beautiful song, I totally relate to the lyrics. Couldn't have described how I used to feel in a better way.

- **This train don't stop here anymore – Elton John.** Whenever I felt that I kept being miserable, low, going over the same stuff I used to play this.

- **Laguna sunrise – Black Sabbath** a slow and melodic song. Gives me joy and calms me I have to be in the right mood to really get it into it.

Some questions to consider . . .

What songs do you love listening to?

Which song makes the hairs on the back of your neck stand up?

Which ones are so beautiful they move you to tears? Any that touch your soul? That you can totally relate to.

What songs change your mood? Lift you? What songs bring you back to a time, a happy moment?

Hope

Sees the invisible, feels intangible,
and achieves the impossible
—www.facebook.com/ beyondyourself09

What is this chapter about?

This isn't about faith or about some Christian beliefs. This is about us. The ability, the skill to believe to have faith in the future. You will be anxiety free!

Hope is something intangible, it can't be seen only felt, but for you to believe that you can do better, to move forward to be better in the future, you have to have it. I will show you some steps on how you too can develop it. If you have hope then this chapter will show you how to improve it further. Without hope, you will not be able to move forward. To have faith you will overcome. That you will strive to go through all the dark days knowing that the future is brighter.

How do I find my hope?

You build it. It starts as something very small and you allow it to blossom. Believe in the impossible! Start with determination and will to achieve then grow it. Knowing that hope is a massive factor in your change is the first step. Hope is not just an emotion but a way of thinking!

What does hope feel like?

This is individual. A feeling that is different for everyone. It's that inner resilience. That thought at the back of your head. Being in a good mood hopeful the events of the day will unfold how you know they will. It's looking forward to the future.

It's not feeling anxious. When I am hopeful I am calm, confident, happy have belief in myself. I have hope all will be okay.

Developing your hope

Having a journal also comes in very handy, helping build and grow your hope as you record your accomplishments. In turn, building your self-confidence.

- **Write down your strengths**. Everyone has strengths and talents write this down. What are your accomplishments?

- **Praise yourself**, celebrate your positive traits.

- **Surround yourself with positive supportive people**. People that will encourage you and make you feel valued. With everything in life more can be achieved with good people than on your own.

- **Role model?** Is there anyone from your friends or family that you could use as an example to help in your accomplishments?

- **How do your friends make you feel?**

- **Do things you enjoy**. By doing things daily that you will enjoy will make you happy and build your hope.

- **Perseverance** – know that many times it won't work but have hope that you can learn from each fall-back and go back again better, stronger.

Be patient and persistent

I have built my hope by writing my achievements down and by reviewing what I have done. I have seen progress, something tangible to hold onto. I have a will to succeed to have a better life for my family and seeing my progress excites me for the future. My only problem now is that I want the future here, right now!

Why have hope?

For you to make changes to go forward, to keep going during the bad times, you need to have hope to know the worst times will go. You can get better. But Hope is something that can't be given. It's something you have to believe, its faith that things can change and be better. They will!

Not to have hope, to feel hopelessness, is one of the saddest parts of anxiety. Because you need spirit and hope to be able to improve your anxiety.

Having hope pushes you beyond your limits. It gets you to believe that everything will work out okay.

Better things are coming. Have hope!

This chapter in a nutshell

- Believe in yourself—be patient, be persistent. Expect to fail, learn from your failures, see why it didn't work out and drive forward.

- For you to get better you must have hope. You must develop your hope. Hope is a skill that you have to learn.

- Keep a grateful diary, list three things you are grateful for each day.

- Write a list of your accomplishments—celebrate them. Even the small things.

The Power of Resilience

'She stood in the storm,
And when the wind did not blow her away,
She adjusted her sails'.
—Elizabeth Edwards

What is in this chapter?

Resilience is another important skill to move you towards a stronger you and a better life. This chapter explains what you need and ways to build your resilience. What is resilience? How do you improve it?

What is resilience?

The dictionary definition is described as 'the capacity to recover quickly from difficulties; toughness'.

To become resilient, you need different skills and requires different sources of help. These include rational thinking, physical and mental health, and good relationships with those close to you.

Resilience isn't just about the huge setbacks; it's dealing with the small big things. The challenges we face. We do have some resilience, but to form strong resilience according to the skillsyouneed.com there are four basic ingredients:

1 – **Awareness** – being aware of your self-talk and what's going on around you.

2 – **Thinking** – able to understand and interpret events going on in a rational, balanced way.

3 – **Asking** for help – reach out to others.

4 – **Fitness** – being physically and mentally healthy to face the challenges.

Psychologist Albert Ellis created a simple model, the ABC for adversity, beliefs, and consequences. He describes that if we encounter adversity, it is how we then think about this event that tells us what we do and behave next.

Life doesn't always go according to plan.

Shit happens. I never expected in my life to be involved in an armed robbery. It is the ability to recover quickly from difficult situations. It is the ability to endure and keep going that will stand you out. The cornerstone of taking on your anxiety is your inner resilience.

It gives people the mental strength to cope with stress and hardship. Resilience is a skill that takes time to build up.

I will never forget the time my wife showed me her inner strength and resilience, finding endurance and just sheer will to succeed. We had a difficult childbirth with our first child. She suffered the early stages of labour for a week before the birth, at one stage her pains were every 20 minutes! She was already exhausted before it came to the day. Our daughter was also back to back; it was even more painful than a usual childbirth. When the labour did properly kick in it was still 48 hours before she gave birth. And there was a moment that the gas and air didn't react well to her. That's another story. It got to the end and she was massively struggling, they said that they were going to do ventouse, which my wife just didn't want. She saw where the baby was and said '*no, I can do this*'. And she did a few harder, enduring pushes and our first was born. I had so much admiration for her. The will and endurance despite having nothing left to give, she still pushed on. The agony, the physical and mental exhaustion, and she still achieved.

What does this mean to your anxiety? Well, it shows that with loved ones around you, with hope and belief people encouraging you on, loving you, showing they care, you can bounce back from a lot and come through stronger.

What times have you fought through adversity?

Write it down. This could be a small thing.

Ways to improve your inner resilience.

To overcome, to endure the frustrations and emotional pain anxiety causes, you need to be resilient. Bad things do happen to good people. The difference is not to let it define you. Accept the situation and find ways to make a positive response to what has happened.

This happened to me; I had an awful experience. I had to get a lot worse for me to come through the other side. I wanted to do better, I wanted to use my experiences from the armed robbery, and before to help others that have experienced anxiety.

Some ways of improving your inner resilience

- Looking for the good in all bad situations—you still need to accept the pain and suffering, be hurt but also look at what opportunities that can come about from this. Look for the positive. Sometimes this can be tough, but there is always a positive to find!

- You should be thinking '*I live to learn*'. All of us make mistakes none of us are perfect, but we can do better if we understand we are here to learn. And move forward. A great piece of advice that I picked up from another book was 'consider everyone you meet as a teacher.'

- Open up—be grateful so if this is showing acts of kindness to others or receiving acts. Or opening up to your feelings. Build your own support network.

- Look after yourself.

- See the humour in life.

- Find a sense of purpose.

- Believe in yourself.

This chapter in a nutshell

- Resilience is described as the capacity to recover quickly from bad situations.

- Sometimes bad things happen, it's how you deal with them that defines you as a person.

- You can grow stronger resilience by looking after yourself, having self-confidence.

- Resilience is learned from experience. It is a highly important skill.

Questions, Questions and More Questions!

Some questions for you to consider.

How does anxiety affect you?

What would you say to someone who has anxiety?

What do you think was the experience that started it all?

What experiences have you had?

How have you dealt with your anxiety?

What gives you joy?

What are you grateful for?

What do you like to do in your spare time?

Who inspires you?

What makes you proud?

What gives you hope?

What are your dreams?

What do you think you will get out of meditation?

Some Different Ways of Coping with Anxiety . . .

Blow some bubbles!

This is an excellent idea to calm yourself during an attack. You have to slow down your breathing, having to take deep breaths to blow the bubbles and gives you something to focus your mind. The colours and shapes that come out help you to enjoy them, it is a great way of helping your attack. I love this idea!

Doodle in a notebook

Writing down how you are feeling when anxiety kicks in. Again helps you focus on something else and helps to clear your mind out.

Play with PLAY-DOH

People have said that it helps to focus on your hands then feel the PLAY-DOH. They like to make things with it. Some of the things they have made are beautiful.

Have a bath (and) pamper yourself

Whether it's making just as hot as you like or buying your favourite bath bombs, scents and or candles or just to spend some time chilling. This will relax your muscles, unwind your mind and reduce your daily anxieties. Doing it before bed also sets you up for a good night sleep.

Humming

Hum the tune of your favourite songs can slow down your heart rate. It also relaxes your face, neck, and shoulders.

Snogtastic!

Kissing increases the love hormone, which relaxes us and lowers the stress hormone. It relaxes you in a similar way to meditation, lowering your anxiety and improving your mood! Great stuff. I don't need any more encouragement than that!

Have an orgasm! (my favourite)

Some people have said that it really helps them. Loosens the muscles and relaxes the mind and body.

Laughter

It seems an obvious one yet it is probably the most difficult as you really don't want to be laughing when you are in the throes of a very scary, very real panic attack. But laughter does reduce the stress hormones that come with anxiety. The effects are immediate and reduce anxiety further over time. I have read several articles on this subject. The claim is you don't need medication or a long time to change. Some claim that it can be done in just ten days. A bold claim.

To My Old Self 1

Old me – Does this get any better? I can't breathe my world feels small. I am a total loser. What help am I to anyone? I want out of my life.

New me – Just you wait. Hang in there! What your future holds is going to be great.

Old me – Looks in disbelief 'yeah sure'.

New me – You're going to do things you never believed you would do, or believe possible, you are going to take yourself in a completely different direction. You're going to believe you can beat this! You will learn who you are, you are going to break the cycle of anxiety.

Old me – We have anxiety. Right! I am depressed I just want to be left alone. In my own world.

New me – You will gain hope it will get easier. Just wait and see!

Being Proud

---

*'Be proud of who you are and everything
you have overcome.'*

Using positive affirmations helps to ground me, reassure
me and focus on what I need to do. I have put these
mantras in my book.

Look at your journey so far, look at your life up to this
point. Two-and-a-half years ago I was broken. My
marriage was on the rocks. I didn't like the person I was. I
was despondent. Now, look at me, such a change in view
and life. Almost a different person.

What has your journey been like? What have been your
challenges?

Being proud of yourself is about envisioning the person you want to be and making the best efforts to grow as a person.

Who do you want to be?

I want to make a difference to others. To give others hope that they too can take on anxiety and break free.

What are your passions?

I am proud of what I have done in the past year. To keep going despite the obstacles. The struggle to fight my own fears, what would happen if they hate my book? How do I finance this book? How do I keep writing every day when my job is so exhausting and I don't have the time?

What are you proud of?

I am proud of my family. I am proud of my wife. I am lucky to have someone that has been so selfless and has kept going through everything. I am proud that so many people have come to help me write this book and show great encouragement.

I am proud of the way I am fighting back. To grow to do things completely out of my comfort zone. To drive me to learn what is needed and the will to achieve.

What Inspires You?

---

*'Inspiration is when you are
moved enough to take action'*

What is in this chapter?

I will show you what you need to do in order to be
inspired. There are several ways you can inspire yourself,
small things that make a big difference.

Why do you need to be inspired?

To be inspired, you have to dream. To have to believe that
you can make your dreams a reality!

For you to become the best you, you have to feel inspired!
Willing to break new ground, do things you never dreamed

you would do. It opens doors in your mind. To free your mind to new possibilities is amazing, this will inspire you to go further and in different paths.

I am in my 40s now, I still dare to dream. I am on my way to make my dreams happen.

Who is your role model?

Someone to aspire to? I have a few people. My role models have changed as I have got older. People that I aspire to achieve what they have done.

Each person fits into why I have chosen them.

Susan Cain, her book on introverts made me see myself differently. Many TED talks, interviews and Google videos, I see what she is trying to do. To show that in an extrovert world introverts are just as important. Ways of helping both parts of humans shine. Helped me see who I am. Inspiring.

Joanna Penn, what she has done taking a successful business career and moved over to make a success of her writing and business. She has shown her mistakes and her success. It has helped me learn a lot of what the pitfalls are and what I need to do to achieve.

Steve Jobs, a man that believed that he could achieve anything. Everyone that was with him believed in his vision. His team went way further than any other company. They came up with ideas and the rest followed.

Have you anyone in your life that you admire, aspire to be like?

It is important to note that the focus is to be the best you. By learning from others, things we want to improve in ourselves it can inspire us to do better.

How can you be inspired in everyday life?

- Read books, biographies that inspire you. Books of people that have had amazing lives. Richard Branson . . . Steve Jobs for me, but what books for you? Get into their minds, see their mindsets. Understand what motivates them to use that in your own life. It will change how you think.

- Practice more—to become a master you need to make it a daily habit.

- Don't waste time on the past. You can'tdo anything about it. Learn from it and move on.

- Write your obituary. Yes, it's morbid, but it also helps you to focus. Think about death, what do you want to be remembered for? Life is so fleeting, what difference do you want to make?

- The pace of everyday life is exhausting and requires days where I chill out and slow down. Pick up a good book or have duvets days as a family. My favourite time is sitting down in our PJs, duvets over us watching TV or talking to each other. This is when I experience joy. This is what life is about. Enjoying each other's company.

I love taking my dog out for a walk, the stars out, a chance to reflect on the day and watch my dog roam about and have his own adventure.

I feel that I have wasted so much time. Doing things that didn't matter. Worrying about things that weren't worth it and not appreciating what I have.

That I am now playing catch up. Making up for lost time. My battles are with finding time with my family. When I am not feeling exhausted.

I am so lucky I have a wife that loves me. Children that just want to spend time with me and I have two great families.

I want to show my children and be the best role model that I can be. I want my wife to look at me like I do her.

I want to help people. I love seeing people happy. I have spent so much time wasting stuck in my own world. I have suppressed my own instincts for too long. So caught up, so lost! Not able to see the amazing people I have in front of me.

To see people grow and improve when I have had a hand in it fills me with pride. I want everyone to be happy to do better. Seeing that makes me proud.

This book is the continuing of my progress. I have seen so many people that struggle with anxiety I want to show them what you can achieve. What anyone can achieve. I have messed up so many times I have felt a failure, not being able to provide for my family, not being able to be the emotional support for my wife. Not being around when I am needed. It has hurt me. But I have a second chance.

Seeing my better relationship with my family spurs me on, noticing the progress I have made. Not caring so much about what others think and continuing to be the driven person I am.

I also get inspired seeing other's progress, watching their progress journeys they have done. In my retail job, I get to see this a lot. It's their determination and willingness to learn that keeps me in the job.

Triumphing over adversity.

When have you struggled, but you have still achieved?

A few more questions to consider

What inspires you?

What makes you sit up and think I can do this?

This chapter in a nutshell

- Being inspired gives you the determination to break down your own barriers.

- Have a role model, someone, you can aspire to be like. You could have several for different things.

- Ways to inspire yourself to think differently—read a book, practice on improving, and write an obituary about yourself. This will show you what your purpose is in life, what you want it to be!

- Look after yourself

- Think about the things that inspire you. The little things.

To My Younger Self 2

Me now – (looks exhausted) you've got some difficult few weeks coming up. You're going to get as low as you have felt for months but your inner steel now is going to help.

I am going to warn you your anxiety attacks are back, I have had a few awful ones recently. But I know now that this is only temporary.

You will keep ploughing through this book despite your self-doubt and you are going to make some bold decisions, trusting your intuition.

You are going to make some long-lasting friendships and you're going to take a leap of faith into the unknown. You would never have done this two years ago.

Newish Me – So we are continuing to get better?

Me now – I think so.

Newish me – Got to get that book finished though.

Me now – It's almost there! And we are going to afford to pay for an editor, too.

Newish me – See! Miracles do happen!!

Laughter

---

*'The human body is 80% water, so we are
basically just cucumbers with Anxiety'*
—*The Mind Machine*

What's in this chapter?

You will understand why laughter is so important and
helpful to your battle. See ways of improving your mood,
even smiling will improve your relationship with others
and yourself. Move you away from more negative mind
talk. Surprisingly, laughter is a skill that can be learned.

To laugh or not to laugh, that is the question.

Why laugh? Anxiety is a serious business!

Anxiety isn't a laughing matter but laughter can be a massive release. The human brain responds very well to laughter and smiling. It generates feel-good chemicals. The brain even responds when you smile to yourself in the mirror! (Finally, I have an excuse for spending all my days looking in the mirror. I am helping my anxiety!)

Through this you can change your thoughts, your body behaviours and your mental state as all your physical functions are related to each other.

There are several YouTubers that encourage you to laugh for no real reason. I feel really uncomfortable doing this so won't recommend that. It feels false. Hollow. Much better to laugh because you find something funny.

The biggest battle with anxiety will be allowing ourselves to laugh, to feel you can let go. There will be times you will find humour in the moment and laugh.

How do you improve your mood?

If it's a funny film, your favourite sit-com (mine is Big Bang Theory) favourite funny show (mine is play to the whistle), podcasts, funny books, YouTube videos or people you like to let your hair down with, then there are so many benefits to laughter. Even just being silly can be enough. Whatever you find funny is what matters.

This is just some of the short-term benefits

- You feel more relaxed—decreasing your heart and blood pressure. Laughing stimulates circulation and aids muscle relaxation.

- If you are having fun in a group, the bonding and the joining together builds relationships. Helping you feel better about yourself.

- Our family have banter and laugh with each other, it has helped us during adversity and has made a very close group, even when we haven't seen each other for days.

Long-term benefits

- Positive thoughts make chemical reactions in the brain that will help fight anxiety

- Laughter helps to improve dealing with difficult situations and improve your mood, lessening your anxiety, making you feel happier.

Ways to improve your humour

This one is difficult for me, I don't have one!

- Schedule your day to make laughter breaks, take a step out of your routine, find something you can think of that you find funny. This only needs to be for 5 minutes.

- What makes you laugh? What do you find funny?

- Allow yourself to let go. Find somewhere on your own if you don't feel comfortable.

By making this a practice you might be able to replace your anxiety over time instead with a sense of fun or enjoyment.

What does laughter feel like?

Feeling happy, a sense of euphoria feels warm you feel healthier. To truly open up your feelings, to see the fun in life.

A good barrel laugh, the best are to laugh and joke with other people. After a good laugh, I always notice people having their sparkle back. It gives people a massive boost and helps you take on the day. When was the last time you laughed so hard that your stomach ached?

This chapter in a nutshell

- Laughter is one of the most important skills (yes, it is a skill, especially with anxiety) you can have in your journey to be a better you.

- Find time during your day to laugh. Even if this is for just five minutes. Do this by finding things you find funny, whether it's a book or programme on TV.

- Laughter has short-term and long-term benefits. From just making you feel more relaxed to helping to change your mind talk to be more positive. The key is allowing yourself to let go.

Joy

Life's hard
Choose joy anyway
—the house of Hendrix

What's in this chapter?

I want you to see that you can develop joy. Developing joy improves your wellbeing and helps to improve your emotional state. What is it? How can you develop and nurture it? And how it will help you in your battles with anxiety?

Feeling of Joy

A few descriptions—delight, jubilation, triumph, exhilaration, glee, ecstasy, euphoria. Bliss.

What is Joy?

Joy is described by the Webster's dictionary as 'to experience great pleasure or delight.' That to me is joy.

I describe my joy as little pockets—very fleeting and most of the time it's the small things that give me joy. Joy isn't a state, being joyful all the time leads to happiness.

'Joyful bonds create our identity, our ability to act like ourselves in distress and our capacity to face pain'
—DEVELOPING JOY STRENGTH AND OUR CAPACITY TO PERSEVERE –
Dr E James Wilder

There are times in life when you are joyful. Birth of a child, your wedding and sexual relationships are good examples.

Joy is described by Gill Bolte Taylor from her TED Talk as a choice. Joy is a learned skill, something we are not born with!

How do I develop joy?

- **Stop comparing yourself to other people**. This leads to anger, frustration, and envy. Focus on being the best you. Getting you better. Other people have their own battles to beat. You don't see that, you only see what is on the outside and compare that to yourself. You can only do better from yourself. It's the best way to go forward.

- **Mindful meditate.**

- **Pursue meaningful goals**.

- **Share**. If it's sharing your money, time or your feelings. Only you will know what the biggest thing you need to do is. In my case, it's more time to others. I have already been working on sharing my feelings.

- **Mind talk**. Meditation, helps you work on this but this is a key point to focus on. Be kind and considerate to yourself. Watch what you say, this will be the difference to what path you go down, joy or despair.

- **Be creative and expressive**. Play for the sake of playing. I have mentioned this in previous chapters but it stimulates our brain allowing us to be free of stress and pain. Find your bliss.

- **Spend time in the natural world**. Take in your surrounds, find beauty in the everyday. I take my dog for a walk and look up at the stars. I love going out to my garden and seeing my flowers grow. It makes me feel peace with the world. Enjoy the present.

- **Gratitude**. Appreciate things part of your mindful meditation. Appreciate the small things. We are so conditioned to want more, to strive for more things. We don't appreciate what we have and what is going on in the here and now. Using your gratitude journal and practice.

- **Listen to music**. There are some songs that move me. What songs that you love to listen to?

- **Don't worry**. On average you have 60,000 thoughts a day. If you have had a bad day don't dwell on them. Hold onto a memory or something you are looking forward to in the future.

- **Create a bliss board**. I love this one. Take a large sheet of cardboard. Find somewhere in your home that you often see. Fill it with captions, words, and pictures that you want for your life. This gives you focus, inspires you and shows you the way. Putting you in a good mood to start off your day. It has to be personal to you. If not, then perhaps go onto Pinterest and pin up your own section to inspire you.

- **Challenge yourself**. Get out of your comfort zone, push yourself to do something you have really wanted to do. But we're afraid to do. Now is the time to do it!

- **Deal with sadness**. This is excellent advice. Find a place where you can be alone. Tell yourself 'I am fine. I feel sad, I just need to cry.' Don't focus on the negative feelings. Doing this clears out the sadness. Many have described at being joyful afterward, and relieved. Bottling your sadness up isn't healthy. Trust me on that one. Without dealing with your sadness you will block the joy in to your life. By numbing the dark emotions we also numb the light. In order to feel joy, you have to feel the dark too.

What does it feel like?

I would describe my experiences as little pockets of euphoria. Joy is fleeting, but by appreciating the little things you will be surprised how many times it jumps out at you. Surprise! It is intense. It is beautiful.

Why have joy?

To have joy in yourselfleads to happiness. I have small pockets of joy jump up on me from time to time during my day. Thanks largely to my mindfulness meditation, I can feel them far more vividly than I ever have. I can't think of a time previous I have experienced these small moments. They are intense and amazing. They are a break away from my anxiety.

When was the last time you felt joy?

Driving home last night, a long day, felt stressful and anxious as I was late picking my son up. I was going over my day not feeling that I had accomplished everything and worrying that I had missed something really important. Then I looked out my window as the sun was going down, the clouds in the sky and the beautiful oranges and yellows lit up the horizon. It was beautiful. I felt a flush of joy, made me realise how unimportant my thoughts were, and made me smile.

Describe below how you last felt it.

What did you see, touch, feel and smell?

What was it that made you feel this?

What is your joy?

Joy, for me, isn't the huge things. It's the little things. Like—

I love going to bookshops, the freshness and soft feel of the covers. The pressed clean look, just ready to be opened. The endless possibilities . . .

They call me, demanding to be heard, inspiring books from the minds of brilliant people. The chance to get an insight into their lives, what drives them. The smell, I keep my books wrapped up, making sure they aren't ruined— dog-eared and don't open them fully to ensure their newness for as long as possible.

Getting into a clean bed, crispy sheets. After a long, hard day, the feeling laying there smelling the fresh linen, the feeling of relaxing and calm the comfortable pleasant feeling on your body. Just to lay there and appreciate it. Is awesome!

Taking my dog for a walk at night with the stars out. After a long day just to be on my own with my dog. The breeze on my face, the birds singing. Allowing myself to relax, with my thoughts—chewing over the day and enjoying this time. Watching the sun set in all its beautiful colour.

It's your children giving you an unexpected hug. Just because they want to. It's sitting down together for dinner. To discuss your day. To just be a family, even if it's a brief, few moments.

It's looking into your wife's eyes with no words needed and knowing exactly what she is thinking. It's cuddling up together in bed—precious moments.

It's noticing something of great beauty a landscape or the light on a hill. It's spotting a flower in my garden that has just come out. It's having banter with my family and friends. It's feeling a cool light breeze on my face during a hot day. It's seeing people happy. It's seeing friends and family grow and develop into the people I know they can be. That's my joy.

What is your joy?

What makes you happy??

Find out what gives you joy and do it.

This chapter in a nutshell

- Joy is delight, jubilation, bliss.

- Having joy helps us face pain, improves our well-being and gives us a more positive outlook.

- You can develop joy by meditation, to have a cry to wash away the sadness without focusing on the negative feelings.

- To focus on changing your future and by working on your self-talk.

- Joy is contagious.

220

From Superpowers and Beyond!

I have anxiety, and I have superpowers!

What is in this chapter?

We will discuss what they are. What you can do to use them now and how they can be a massive asset in the future. Using these superpowers to be your better you.

Superpowers, really?!

Did you know that you have superpowers? Yep, it's true. There are four superpowers you gain when you fight anxiety.

We all know the difficulties we face. But there is scientific evidence that we also benefit from anxiety.

What superpowers do I have?

Survival mode

Three French scientists (El Zein, Wyart, and Grezes) in their studies have found that people with anxiety are able to detect threats in just 200 milliseconds.

That's quick! Far quicker than other human beings without anxiety. A world-class baseball player takes 400 milliseconds to decide what to do when the ball is pitched. We decide threats in HALF THAT TIME!

Increased IQ

Researchers at SUNY Downstate medical center found that as we Overanalyse our environment, we need our brains to constantly process information. For our brains to do this we need a higher IQ! We need more capacity.

Increased empathic ability

According to research from psychologists at the department of psychology at the University of Haifa, Israel we 'exhibited elevated empathic tendencies.' We could not only have empathic tendencies but could read other people's emotions with a high level of accuracy.

Iron will determination to keep going

Every day we cope with anxiety. We keep fighting. Despite knowing how tough it feels. We keep going, we do it anyway. Our iron will just to appear normal is a colossal superpower!

What can I do with these superpowers?

Higher emotional intelligence helps you be a better leader. It has me. I see the subtle things that people do, that others miss.

Use them to drive yourself forward. What we deal with every day we can use to help us break free of anxiety. We have discussed the skills you need in previous chapters.

You can reach out to talk, to be a support, and help others and yourself at the same time. That feeling of empowerment you will get by doing a good deed the feeling you aren't alone and build your self-confidence will greatly enhance your chances of breaking free of anxiety just from this!

What about for the future? Could these superpowers actually enhance my life after the worse times of anxiety? Yes, it can.

A higher IQ to process all the information can be used to gather different information rather than fears, worries and overthinking. What about reading? Learning? The development of yourself. I am not a doctor but I have found that I can use my improved 'higher intelligence' to improve and develop myself more. Expanding my mind to more possibilities. I have found I am more open to different concepts and I feel I see the world very differently to others.

Better emotional intelligence means that you can get on and care about others. This is an awesome skill to have. One that many people will love to have themselves, you can use it to build stronger, deeper friendships and relationships. It will also help you improve your leadership skills. Having high emotional intelligence is one of the most important skills you need in today's business. But, so few people have it. You will have it in abundance!

Having an iron will to keep going, to stay focused is a superpower that has time and again bailed me out when writing this book and enhanced my career recently.

That steadfast refusal to give in, to keep going despite how you feel and against all odds. That's rare and highly sought after!

Your future!

Think about this for a moment. How you feel now, what you deal with can be a massive advantage in the future if you continue to move yourself forward.

Smashing anxiety is one hell of an effort, but to do it will help you be a more balanced person. Be able to help and lead others. Be focused and driven towards your goals and determination to be a better you.

All through your anxiety! All through the pain and suffering that you face. It could seriously enhance your life if you let it.

In my career since the armed robbery, I have gone from wanting to end my life to becoming a highly sought after manager. I have worked hard to improve me, we have improved our marriage and I have improved relationships. I feel I am a better person since. I feel I am far stronger and have a bigger edge since the robbery. That's through using my superpowers.

Imagine that. Your suffering could mean a lot more than you could ever expect!

A better life, a life you will love, a better you!

This chapter in a nutshell

- It has very recently been proven from studies that we have superpowers from our anxiety.

- Through our suffering we gain increased IQ, can assess threats faster than a world-class baseball player can decide how to hit a ball, iron will to keep going despite wanting to completely give in, and extremely high levels of emotional intelligence.

- You can use these superpowers to enhance your life now and to use them in the future to become your best you.

- Your suffering can be worth something very valuable to you!

ATARAXIA

A state of freedom from emotional
disturbance and anxiety; tranquillity
—Dictionary.com

My Friends' Stories

*You aren't alone
There is hope!*

What is this chapter about?

This is a compilation of people's personal stories with anxiety. What they have to deal with and any advice they want to give to others that are suffering. They are their own words so I have done all I can to ensure their words and left as it is. The names have been changed but the stories are real.

They have poured out their feelings, their hurts, and worries. They have done this to help you, to inspire you. They too have suffered.

James' story

'. . . when the job of your dreams changed, it made me not want to get to work anymore. Sadly I started to rely on alcohol to help me sleep which put a lot of pressure on my family.

I am currently looking for work elsewhere and have stopped drinking at silly times. Anxiety is a massive part of this and still is in the main.

I have an understanding GP who I have seen a few times, and they always refer to a helpline called Lifeline.

. . . I won't be going down that route as I have a strong support network at home. But for other people, it is always an option.

I am coming out good, on the other side thank goodness.

Jenna's story

I will avoid driving more than 50 miles away from home. Hate not knowing where I am not going! Hate traveling or going anywhere new on my own! It's okay to have anxiety most people do!

I managed to avoid any bad experiences! Unless I have blocked them out! I would, however, deal with it by my faith and a lot of pre-planning!!

Motherhood I was very different (bad experience with the ex). He destroyed a part of me as I gave everything to my daughter and neglected myself. I found routine was a safe option and the only way to cope with it I guess.

I now have been a single mum for 20 years, and some habits are hard to break. My friend has offered to pay for me to go to Belgium but I like my bubble too much. Call me boring, but it's safe. I have been to dark places I never want to go back to. Without my faith and now my workmates it could happen. I pray every day, that is my medicine. If I am meant to go to Belgium, I will, or my anxiety is good and keeping me here for a reason.

Becca's story

Anxiety has played a big part of my life for ten years. I went from being very popular, happy, social and confident to now—unable to face social events with the kids or friends.

I can't travel or leave my house on my own, making holding down a job impossible. My anxiety causes me to get all sweaty, emotionally and physically sick. I get anxious just thinking about doing the slightest task.

To someone suffering from anxiety to say it's okay to feel like this. You are not alone and just remember it can't hurt you and help them with deep breathing tricks.

The very first time I had experienced anxiety I had just given birth to our 3rd child . . . within minutes his dad, my partner at the time confessed to having an affair. My heart began racing, getting all clammy, struggling to breathe and getting a knotted stomach which caused me to be sick. This feeling went on for months, even over the smallest thing. Just taking my baby for a walk would trigger it again.

I had tried dealing with it by getting self-help books, counselling, and yoga. But my son's dad became very mentally abusing. He seemed to enjoy seeing me suffer so wouldn't let me leave the house.

The anxiety got so bad I became suicidal. I spent six months being physically sick due to being constantly anxious. I was bed bound, lost so much weight that my seven year old weighed more than me. My friends soon lost interest. I was anxious over everything—caught in a vicious cycle.

I couldn't take any more. After a spell in hospital, I knew I had to do something. My son's dad had given up on me and was having affairs all the time, I was missing out on the kids growing up—they needed me.

I began taking medication to get me through each day. I saw a slight improvement over time, but still, anxiety was there. I wanted it gone, so I began counselling. I opened up to my therapist, starting with my childhood, which wasn't a good one!! She believed that my anxiety stemmed from such a bad childhood but I was always trying to be so strong and carry on, that after the birth of my son and his dad's confession it took me over the edge . . .

When I was at my lowest, I felt that everyone was better off without me as I was useless. I just hid in my room 24/7. Crying all the time. I couldn't face simple tasks like cooking or bathing as I'd be so anxious if I had a bath I felt like just drowning myself. I was scared of what was happening to me. I didn't like it. I felt like I belonged in a mental hospital.

My son's dad took my son and moved away with him. I didn't see him for months. I knew I had to fight this. I would force myself to get up in the mornings and sit in the living room for short periods of time. I know it sounds silly (MY NOTE—not at all silly. An amazing achievement!) But it was an achievement for me. It was doing that for a week or so I could start doing other things like watching tv and I found that I started getting dressed. The real turning point for me was being allowed to see my son at school. I knew how much I missed him and knew I had to leave the house to see him. I was so anxious walking up to the school . . . but I did it.

His face, when he saw me standing at the school gates, was amazing—he ran right up to me and gave me the biggest hug ever!! We both cried.

Walking home after seeing him I was so happy, not just the fact that I got to see my son but I managed to leave the house on my own! Something I felt I would never be able to do.

It's my kids that keep me going. They are a great support even though they do the usual kid stuff—nothing different. I know deep down that they need me just as much as I need them.

I'm still suffering from anxiety to this day but I have found ways of coping with it better. I wear a rubber band on my wrist and whenever I begin to feel anxious I ping it many times until the pain takes me off that anxious feeling. Plus I still take medication.

I know now just to take each day as it comes. I know some will be good, others will be bad.

Chloe's story

I have felt anxious for as long as I can remember. Some anxious episodes have no obvious reason. Others do, eg work. And others are totally unreasonable, eg my partner had taken longer in town than he said he would, so I think something terrible has happened to him—he's crashed, been stabbed (my mind will elaborate on these ideas too, such as his phone was stolen when stabbed, which is why no one rung me) and when he is back I beat myself up for such stupid thoughts.

When I feel anxious without any obvious reason I am very restless and alert—trying to take my mind off things by doing the housework etc and looking out the windows all the time.

I worry about people I don't know, issues that don't impact me immediately (things on the news) and I am ridiculously paranoid. I won't talk on the phone to people I don't know. In fact, I only talk to my grandparents and my partner on the phone—I use email or write if I ever need to communicate with someone directly, only order takeaway online.

Going anywhere new is a nightmare for me. If it's a holiday/trip I have to psych myself up for days in advance. I hate driving places that I haven't been to before and I personally only drive alone to the same few places, my partner drives me to others or I don't go at all.

Relationships with friends are often hard, although they are amazing and understanding what I am like. If I haven't heard from them in a while I worry it's because they don't want to be friends, when they get in touch I question why in my head, when we are out I worry I will say the wrong thing or something stupid.

Anxiety, depression and paranoia have all merged into one.

I suffer with a hair-pulling condition, which is linked to anxiety. I have frequent migraines and heartburn, as well as daily heart palpitations for which I had an ECG—came back clear and was put down to anxiety.

On the plus side I haven't had an anxiety attack for 18 months.

(What would you say to someone that has anxiety?)

I couldn't offer advice, I could only talk about our experiences.

I think my parent's separation at 12 started everything— lots of 'secrets' and information that had been withheld from me suddenly came to light and began to doubt everyone and everything that was said to me.

My mother had postnatal depression after having me, then again six years later when my second brother—family members have often said that my mum took things out on me, especially as my dad often worked away.

I have had a number of cheating partners. One partner took money from me, was physically, emotionally and mentally abusive. Attempted suicide.

I was chucked out aged 12 and went to live with my dad and his mistress; a woman closer to my age than his. Things were very bad in that house and I wasn't treated very well by my step mum and my father always sided with her. I was taken to my grandparents to stay for months at a time.

I have had counselling, although it didn't feel it helped at all. Taking Prozac-based medication, which takes some of the underlying anxiety away. I write things down that are on my mind. I brought a dog (yay). Try to adapt a 'if I can do something about it now do it, if I can't do anything don't worry'. The don't worry part is easier said than done.

There is such a stigma around mental health. As well, I think that unless you are visibly quite mentally ill, people think you should just 'toughen up' and 'get on with it'. Anxiety is so exhausting. The fact that I am still here, living my life with all the positives in it, is proof that I (and others suffering with anxiety) are some of the toughest people on god's earth.

Helen's story

There are days when I just can't go shopping when I need to—busyness and the people. There are times where we have planned for us to go out but I just can't do it. I can't face it. My partner is really understanding.

When I have interviews I need to know where the window is and need to be close to the door or I will get anxious. I know I won't sleep the night before because I will be thinking a lot of what could happen.

But I can use my anxiousness to drive me my nervous energy. It will keep me going.

I have also been in on two occasions to check what they are wearing to ensure I have the correct dress code for my new job. I get too obsessive when I go to the gym. I push myself way too hard and obsess about it. When I am really stressed I go running. It hurts so much when I stop it is a relief. So I don't focus on my anxiety. It's a good distraction.

My anxiety is in obsessive compulsive-disorder (OCD). I will always think of the worst thing that can happen and plan for it. So that if it doesn't happen I won't be anxious I will have a plan. The worst thing that can ever happen. When I am sorting kids out I will always have a backup if one person is ill. The last few weeks have been difficult as I haven't got a job, I need a purpose. And this has made things difficult.

That the biggest things is that you are not on your own, more people experience it than you know. There isn't a cure for it. Medication helps but it will then eventually get used to it. Then then there are side effects. You may feel out of it, like others won't understand. They will. We are a lot stronger than we think. To battle this every day. We have to be strong to hide it. You don't overcome anxiety but learn to use it.

When I was at my lowest I would put some clothes over my pjs, take kids to school then come home and get back into bed. Couldn't do anything else. All the energy I had for that day went into picking up and taking my kids.

I have a dog, it is important for my downtime. I have daily walks, it helps me. It is a chance to give me time to myself and to get into a routine. We also go out and spend time as a family take the dog for a walk. There is always someone worse off than you.

I am in love for the first time, I have never felt like this before. I want to love and trust again. Now I feel valued and respected, something I never had in the past. It was like I was lucky to have them. I feel the opposite now, lucky to have each other. When I am having some time on my own (needing some headspace) and the kids come back with him and they are laughing and joking, I feel joy.

I would say that I have always been anxious as was my family. No one different thing brought it forward. I have always been like it. Can't think when it was. Always feeling can I fit in? Am I good enough? The pressure to be liked. Getting nervous, trying to be normal. I worked harder to fit in. I felt on the outside but my friends said when we were talking I was always the one in the centre of it all.

When I was younger I used to be deliberately sick, it was my way of being in control. I would regularly do this.

I will write down notes in the middle of the night if something comes to me, I jot it in a notebook even if I can't read it. It helps me clear my mind. Declutter.

I have been having operations and it has been sending my moods all over the place. I have used my own experiences to help me. I have said to myself I have been in a wheelchair for four months, not knowing if I will walk again, I can deal with this!

I have taken medication for it. It helped me I wasn't feeling lows, not feeling highs either. I had made so many changes and wasn't feeling benefit. They were supportive of me when I came off of it.

A few things to consider

What's your story?

What do you tell yourself that stops you from making a difference in your life?

What scares you to your core, but you would love to do?

What story do you say to yourself that prevents you from daring to do better?

What holds you back?

Everyone has a story they say to themselves, what's yours?

SOPHROSYNE

A healthy state of mind, Characterised by
self-control, moderation, and a deep awareness of
one's true self, and resulting in true happiness.

INSOUCIANT

Free from concern, worry, or anxiety; nonchalant.
—Dictionary.com

Life develops what it demands..
the toughest path creates the
strongest warrior.....

Pray not for
lighter load,

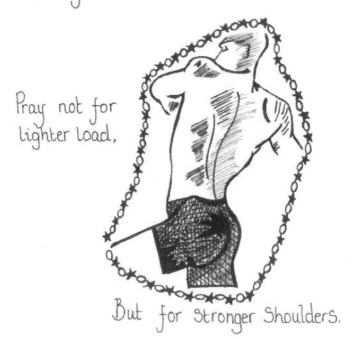

But for stronger Shoulders.

The Abyss—My Darkness

I have spent a lifetime of pain stuck in the abyss, with no light to guide me.

I have clawed up to the rim, fingernail by fingernail. Every second has felt like an eternity, living a life of hell. Not knowing what I was facing.

I have suffered, I have endured, I have felt lost and broken. Not deserving of love or happiness. All too often willing to sabotage what little good I have got.

I have felt it a curse, a humiliation of never feeling good enough.

The abyss, my darkness was my enemy, it anchored me, unable to escape. I was desperate, crushed and alone . . .

I haven't escaped the abyss; it stays by my side now, always telling me I am useless and not good enough. I observe these as only my thoughts.

My darkness reminds me that life is amazing, that you have seen the worse from life, from people. But you can also see the good.

It reminds me how important every moment is. It has shown me pain; now I see joy. See the appreciation of my world and my loved ones. To show my vulnerability and pain to help others.

I have never felt joy as intensely as I do now. My darkness drives me on, giving me the courage to face my fears. I am no longer desperate for my darkness to leave, but to be with me as I head towards the light.

My darkness reminds me how far I have come, and how much further I need to travel. I need my darkness by my side to be able to be my better me.

The Humber Bridge

Showing how much I have improved—Another milestone achieved!

I was taking a journey to Hull as part of my training very recently.

Off in the distance, I saw a huge bridge. The sun caught the giant columns making them appear white. I looked out over the river as I got closer I thought wow that's captivating!

Then the sudden realisation hit me. *Oh my god I am going to have to drive over that!* A wave of blind panic and terror hit me. I could feel the start of an attack. The knots building in my stomach, the light feeling in my chest and head. I used my 7/11 technique and said to myself let's feel all my emotions and thoughts. Keeping myself anchored on my breath, I allowed them all to come at me . . . *Just as you get on the bridge there could be a terrorist attack and blow up the bridge! You will die! Those struts could come off, and the bridge could collapse! That's you a goner! What happens if you don't drive well and accidentally drive into the sea? It looks too tight for cars! What a way to die. Drowning in the river!* I went to note them, but I realised I was smiling! My panic, my worry had dissipated. I was smiling at my own thoughts!

I got to the bridge and drove over it. I scanned over at the river below and took the whole view in; the huge river below almost looked like a sea the countryside surrounding it. The families were walking together on the bridge and smiling. I took in the whole moment. Doing my 7/11 taking in all the beauty. It was a beautiful moment.

Once I had parked up a short distance later. I reflected on what had just happened. Even six months ago I would have had a panic attack. I would have driven over it, but I would have been scared witless. Now a massive milestone had been reached. Another important moment in my battle over anxiety. I had retaken control. I am pushing my anxiety back. I was so proud of myself! I made sure I celebrated this moment. I bought myself a chocolate bar. That's how I roll!

I have learned of late that the feelings of fear don't mean anything. My emotions cannot predict the future. If I feel, fear it's just an emotion. One to be tackled.

I felt elated. Yes! I thought. I can't believe it. I smiled at my thoughts.

That feeling of joy for the landscape and view. That elation for not having an anxiety attack—feeling less of a prisoner, made me feel on cloud 9 for the rest of the day. I felt more self-confident. Building my hope more that I am going to be anxiety free soon.

A Reminder of the Man I Was

I recently had a night with little sleep. The following day was tough. My negative mind talk was back. Battering me all day. *You are a failure.* You *are a fraud. Why are you doing this? You aren't good enough. Why are you even trying? Just give up.* I used my breathing to keep me calm. I listened to all the negative talk. My anxiety I could feel close to my chest. Threatening to break out.

I was so grateful for this day because it gave me an insight in to how I used to feel! It taught me how much I struggled, how far I have come and a new found respect for the old me. My journal explained my feelings but to feel them again was powerful.

I have the utmost respect for you that deal with anxiety. My arrogance expects more of myself. Not having the same expectations for others than I do myself. I have spoken about this in a previous chapter.

I now have ways to cope with my anxiety. In the not too distant past, I didn't. I just kept fighting on. I just got punched around all day. Feeling low, feeling insecure, bereft of hope and any self-confidence.

This day gave me another teaching. To learn to forgive. To forgive the person I was. To not be so hard on him. To feel he wasn't good enough. To be proud of him that he kept fighting on. Like I do with every single one of you.

The next day I felt happy all day. I felt relief. I had carried this baggage for a long time. To let it go took a weight away.

I wasn't that bad a man. I battled anxiety. And I got through it.

Just like you will. Learn to forgive yourself.

End Credits—On to Living the Life You Will Love and Become a Better You

---

'Even the darkest night will end,
and the sun will rise.'
—*VICTOR HUGO*—*Les Miserable*

You are now at the end of this book. Well done, you did it!

This book has been a labour of love, and I have written down everything to inspire you to take on anxiety and break free.

I am still on the journey pushing myself forward. I haven't had an anxiety attack since Brighton over seven months ago!

I still get anxious, and I worry. I know that I am on my path to recovery. The homeward straight.

Strangely I feel that it has helped me. To get everything down in print has been my therapy and bringing me closer to my dream.

That can only be exciting!

The experience I have endured. In many books, I have read the author starts off with their struggles and pains, long term it helps them. It's a reminder of what the worse can bring; it's a reminder to appreciate what you have. Only through struggle do you fully grow.

I have been told that I am one of the most determined, driven person they have met. I have goals that I will complete. I have a vision I will achieve.

I am proud of the progress I have made, but I know that there is a lot more I need to do. Little footsteps every day.

Some people have beaten this illness, I dream of that time. It will happen for me too. But, I am also patient.

I have gone from struggling to get out of the house, wanting to end it all to now taking on anxiety, pushing it right back, giving it one hell of a hard time and using my pain and suffering to help others. That's something to be proud of!

My progress in the last two years has been down to having anxiety because I have learned to use it and drive myself beyond my limitations.

Life is a journey. Life is amazing. I am so lucky to have a second chance. To look at death face on, to realise how short life is and to believe I can change and see that the only limits there are the ones you put on yourself.

Life is too short. There is so much that I want to do.

I read that some of the most famous people that have made the most profound effects on the world have battled anxiety. I find comfort in the fact that they have used these struggles to spurn them on to do great things. I have found comfort that with anxiety by their side it has helped them to be the inspiration for others.

I intend to keep on pushing myself to do things I would be scared of and couldn't do only a few years ago. I am still scared, anxious, but now I have a new found determination to do it anyway because I have hope. I have faith that things will work out. I will write more books, on anxiety and a few on fiction. I want to write stories; I want to inspire people. I want to continue to give people hope.

Nothing would make me happier seeing you beat your darkness.

I want people to achieve, to be their better them.

I am a very reserved person. I keep my feelings inside, I don't show the real me, but by writing this book I am doing something I would have never imagined to tell my innermost thoughts, my fear of failure, what I think. What more out of my comfort zone can I push myself?

I know I need to show all my fears, to help others and that's what drives me, that's what keeps me going. To show my vulnerability, to show what I deal with every day. I have to show everything; this book won't work without doing that.

I am determined now to push myself beyond my limits.

I have given myself goals. One of them this year was to doing something entirely out of my comfort zone.

The armed robbery was a life defining moment. I have internalised everything. I hated myself for how I have behaved before it, for allowing myself to wallow in my own self-pity. No longer able to help others. Like I used to be. Not being able to cope with anything.

I am so lucky to have a wife that held me up and kept things together when we needed it. Her greatest strength is her sense of humour. To make us both laugh even in the worse times has been a great blessing.

I care deeply about people. I have become more open and willing to show my vulnerability, show that I am sensitive—something I used to get teased and bullied at school. By opening up has helped people to respond to me.

To accept I am human. I have faults.

By doing this, showing my pains and discussing my anxiety has made me closer to my friends, wife, and children. ⎰

You should be proud of yourself for getting this far.

I have met many people with anxiety and their stories have been profoundly moving, the challenges they face. I have been very proud that they have been willing to show their stories, their pain to help others.

You will face challenges, upheaval, and more battles, but short-term pain will end in long-term gain!

What's the next step for you?

You can take all my learnings from this book and use them in your own life, but that desire has to come from you.

I have shown you how to develop confidence, joy, hope, and inner resilience. What inspires you? What makes you proud? How to meditate and what things helped me. These are excellent skills to have, a great way to encourage you to give you the tools so you can move forward. It's about taking back control over your suffering. You know what to do to get out. There is a light at the end of this dark tunnel. But only you can take yourself there. Only you can achieve.

You can see a way forward now and know that if you work at it, with the support of others, that you can break the cycle. You can go onward, there is a future for you that doesn't involve the suffering of anxiety!

How do you do that?

Get to know yourself. Get to know your trigger points. Understand that some days you are going to struggle when you are feeling lost. Read your journal, see the journey. Understand that these days will pass. Treat yourself with compassion and kindness. You are doing your best. Every accomplishment is enormous, another massive step to overcoming anxiety. Celebrate every achievement, even the small ones! It's an important point for me as us anxiety sufferers struggle to be kind to ourselves.

Use this book as a point of reference. Everything in it is designed to give you all the tools, all the skills to help you take on anxiety. Doing it your way. Some parts you may know or may have those skills, that's fine. Reminding you of what you need is just as important.

Reach out to others.

It is something that I have done more recently. I am now in a couple of anxiety groups. I have found it empowering. I have found it a relief that there are others. In even this world, many others battling this putting up a good fight. The support and help that they give make me realise that I am not alone. No judgments, just the opportunity to talk to people suffering. How they are with each other is restoring my faith in humanity. They show compassion, care, and love. Even in the darkest times.

There are several Facebook groups. They are closed groups, giving you the option to talk to others that suffer without the worry of others seeing and there are tens of thousands that talk in it. Giving you the opportunity to either chat if you want to or to lurk and hear other experiences. Allowing you to feel comfortable first before diving in.

Reach out to love ones and close friends, open up about what you are going through. That's a significant step let them see your struggles lean on them and grow.

Take strength from what you have done this far, show the world what you have done and what you are going to be. If there is anything I could give you is it can be overcome? The power is within you.

Have dreams, strive to achieve, you can make it!

There is a quote from theologian Howard Thurman that Brené Brown likes to use.

'Don't ask what the world needs. Ask what makes you come alive, and go do it. Because what the world needs is people who have come alive.'

When I made this change to beat anxiety, I knew that I needed to get myself a plan and do it. You can do it at your own pace. But strive. The only way you can beat anxiety is in you. Your strength, your heart, your desire and willingness to change. I have shown that it is possible. Many others have done too! If you truly believe you can make this work. How much do you want to break the cycle of fear?

For so long I have played it safe, fear has gripped me like a vice, not able to escape the box. Not able to venture away for fear of reprisal. Well, no longer!

I have taken on anxiety at its own game! They say that the best things in life are the other side of fear. That's the place I want to get to! I am getting to.

I am going to tackle this, doing the things I fear the most. First stop, the chance of ridicule by publishing this book!

There will be days you will feel you are going backwards, there will be days that you feel a complete failure, there will be days you think I can't do this, it's impossible!

Then there are days you feel you are cracking it. You feel happier, you feel hope and joy, those small pockets. You will feel amazing. But you will have to struggle still. This isn't a sprint, this is a marathon but hope, faith and resilience will take you over the line. You will beat this. But you will have to make that change yourself.

You have seen now through meditation what your best you is like. At the worst, you have seen glimpses. That must give you heart of what is within you. That must give you hope and encouragement to keep going. It has me. It will you too.

Strive to be the best version of you! Living the life you will love!

You can now reach the point that you can be the person you want to be. To have big dreams and you can decide what your future looks like. Anxiety free!

Your best life is within your grasp and how to get there!

Think about that. The world is so small there are so many options to what you want to do and where you want to go.

The opportunities are limitless. The only limitations are what you put on yourself.

I will finish with my all-time favorite, inspiring quote.

'Let me tell you something you already know,
Life isn't all sunshine and rainbows
Life is a nasty place, and it will beat you down if you
let it. You, me, or nobody gonna hit as hard as life.
But it ain't about how hard ya hit. It's about how
hard you can get hit and keep moving forward. How
much you can take and keep moving forward.
THAT'S HOW WINNING IS DONE!'
—Rocky Balboa

Now go live your life that you want!

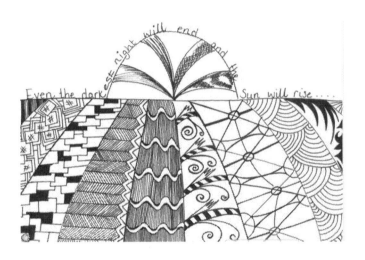

The Best Reading/Anxiety Apps/YouTube Videos

The best apps

Headspace – Guided and unguided meditations, track your progress and choose what you want to improve on. You can decide on everyday mediations, single, or projects.

Calm – Has guided meditations, calming nature pictures and sounds and has a meditation timer. There are some excellent very short meditations. Especially if you need one in an emergency. I would look out for the stories read by a host of well-known stars.

Other Books I have read

THE POWER OF NOW – Egobart Toole

DISCOVER MEDIATION AND MINDFULLNESS – Tara Ward

101 DAYS TO MAKE A CHANGE – Roy Leighton, Emma Kilbey, and Kristina Bill

MINDFULLNESS ON THE GO – Padraig O'Morain

Youtube videos

Inspiring videos

BELIEVE IN YOURSELF – Motivational video

ROCKY BILBOA – inspirational speech

THE MINDSET OF HIGH ACHIEVERS – Best Motivational video for success in life and study 2017

WHEN YOU DO SOMETHING FOR SOMEONE ELSE – Simon Sinek

Anxiety

BE THE WARRIOR, NOT THE WORRIER. FIGHTING ANXIETY AND FEAR – Angela Ceberano

A NEW PLAN FOR ANXIOUS FEELINGS: ESCAPE THE CUSTARD – Neil Hughes

ANXIETY DISORDERS AND PANIC ATTACKS – Alison Sommer

OSCARS SPEECH – Matthew McConaughey winning best actor

Did You Enjoy
Hope over Anxiety?

If you enjoyed this book. I would greatly appreciate it if you could leave me a review on Amazon.

I know your time is precious but it will help me improve this book and my future adventures. It will only take a few minutes to do a sentence or two.

Your feedback will be warmly received.

Thank you,

Christopher Moss

Keeping in Touch

I hope my story helped you, what I do on a day to day basis and the stories of others.

If you want further help and advice. You are more than welcome to visit the following:

Facebook – @CPMossauthor

Facebook group – Hope over Anxiety: Break your anxiety!
Email   –   mosschristopher799@gmail.com
Twitter – @mossyblue

I would love to hear from you about how this book has helped you. I would love to hear your stories.

Coach Call

Would you like further help and guidance? Do you wish to have one to one help from me? I give free first time 30 minute consultations.

Email to contact me. And you can choose a time to suit you.

mosschristopher799@gmail.com

Crisis Centres

AnxietyUK – www.anxietyuk.org

The Sanctuary www.selfhelpservices.org.uk

Rethink mental illness www.rethink.org

No panic www.nopanic.org.uk

Facebook groups

These are all the groups I am a member of. There are much more.

Those you can call on when you need help. They are all closed groups so only those that are in the group can see your posts allowing you to open up and share experiences.

Use the Facebook search engine and put these in . . .

Anxiety and Depression support

Anxiety and depression support group

Let's talk anxiety group

Depression and Anxiety safe haven support group

Me, Myself and anxiety

Acknowledgments

A big thank you to these people. Without their help, this book would not have been possible.

Thank you to Julia Kittscha for her help and support in getting this book edited. Spending hours of her own time to read through my book deserves a medal in itself.

To Dani Foskett for positivity and support when I needed it most.

To Katie Payne for championing my book for believing in me.

To my wife for her support and giving me great advice. For being my second editor.

To Jim Morrelini for his guidance and inspiring me to redo my subtitle.

To everyone in the SPS mastermind community. The best community on Facebook. FACT.

To Ida Fia Sveningsson for taking on a few of my ideas for the book cover, adding her own then taking them to another level. For making the book cover the best I could have ever have imagined!

To Andrea Hill for her awesome illustrations. You rock!

To you reading this. You are the reason I kept going. You are the reason I will keep writing books.

Bibliography

What is anxiety?

Moodjuice.scot.nhs.uk

Anxietyuk.org.uk including studies on anxiety

Nomorepanic.co.uk

Self-confidence

Mindtools.com – building self confidence

Mind.org.uk – self esteem

Brene Brown – the gifts of imperfection

Gratefulness diary

Investing in myself – Huffington post

Life hacker – why should you keep a journal?

What is mindfulness?

Mindfulness on the go – Padraig O'Morain

Mindfulness practice

Mindfulness bible – Dr Patricia Goddard

Mindfulness benefits?

Mindfulness meditation benefits: 20 Reasons why it's good for your mental and physical health – Huffington post

The power of resistance

Skillsyouneed.com – developing resistance

Headspace

Headspace.com

Obituary

Keep any promise – Karim Ishmael

Anxiety and creativity

The gifts of imperfection – Brene Brown

The mindfulness bible – Dr Patricia Collard

Anxietyuk.org – physical exercise and anxiety

Live strong.com – how to build self-confidence and eliminate anxiety

Laughter and anxiety

Help guide.org – laughter is the best medicine

Joy

Mindbodygreen – 7 ways to create more joy in your life

From superpowers to beyond

Provider.com – scientists say that people with anxiety could have superpowers

How we learn – Benedict Carey

Researching crisis centres and best apps

Blessing manifesting

Illustrations by Andrea Hill

Pray for stronger shoulders – words from Dan Millman

Even the darkest night . . . – words from Victor Hugo

Printed in Great Britain
by Amazon